Knock Your Socks Off Prospecting:
How to Cold Call, Get Qualified Leads, and Make More Money

by
William "Skip" Miller
&
Ron Zemke

American Management Association

New York • Atlanta • Brussels • Boston • Chicago • Mexico City • San Francisco
Shanghai • Tokoyo • Toronto • Washington, D.C.

Special discounts on bulk quantities of AMACOM
books are available to corporations, professional
associations, and other organizations. For details,
contact Special Sales Department, AMACOM, a
division of American Management Association,
1601 Broadway, New York, NY 10019.
Tel.: 212-903-8316. Fax: 212-903-8083.
Web site: www.amacombooks.org

*This publication is designed to provide accurate and authoritative
information in regard to the subject matter covered. It is sold with the
understanding that the publisher is not engaged in rendering legal,
accounting, or other professional service. If legal advice or other expert
assistance is required, the services of a competent professional person
should be sought.*

Library of Congress Cataloging-in-Publication Data
Miller, William
*Knock your socks off prospecting : how to cold call, get qualified leads,
and make more money / William "Skip" Miller and Ron Zemke.*
    p. cm.
    Includes bibliographical references and index.
    ISBN 0-8144-7285-0
1. Telephone selling. 2. Selling. I. Zemke, Ron. II. Title.
HF5438.3.M55 2005
658.8'72—dc22   *2005000981*

Artwork © 2005 John Bush.

Printing number

10 9 8 7 6 5 4 3 2 1

Contents

Preface

A true story...

Thomas and Ruddy were a pair of ambitious ten year olds who lived on the same block in Charlotte, North Carolina. Pining for some spending money, they approached their dads with a scheme: Rent us your lawnmowers so we can start a mowing business. A deal was struck and off they went. By August of that hot summer the boys had a dozen accounts apiece—lawns belonging to almost all of the neighbors they knew, most of the lawns within four square blocks, and certainly all of the lawns two ten-year-old boys could handle.

"If we get some other kids," Thomas observed, "we can do even more."

"But we have everyone we know already," said Ruddy.

"I'll bet our dads know a lot of people we can ask," countered Thomas. "And so will the kids we get to help us."

Ruddy, comfortable with his dozen customers, opted out. Thomas recruited two more friends—and their dads' mowers. He got their dads, his dad, and Ruddy's dad to make lists of names and addresses of neighbors the kids didn't know. Then he set off knocking on doors to sign up new mowing clients. Cold calling. Building a book of business from the ground up.

Today Thomas is a college senior. His lawn service boasts 150 clients, seven employees, and an accountant. Some of his clients date back to the beginning. When he graduates, Quality Landscape and Garden Services will be Thomas' full-time occupation.

There is a difference between cold calling and prospecting.

"Cold calling" means hitting the streets to knock on the doors of people you don't know. It means picking up the phone to call people you've never met. Cold calling is part and parcel of the activity called "prospecting," which can begin when you ask people you *do* know for the names and numbers of other people who might, possibly, do business with you. It continues as you pursue these people—gently, carefully—until they either become customers or you determine that their business potential is unlikely or too low.

Knock Your Socks Off Prospecting: How to Cold Call, Get Qualified Leads, and Make More Money is about making the most of your cold-calling opportunities. It is about developing the skill and judgment that lets you know when to pursue a prospect all the way to customer status, and when to cut your losses and move on. In fact, we've tried to make that even easier for you. Throughout the book you will find our sales prospector. When you see this little guy, pay close attention. He'll offer nuggets of wisdom that will help you find gold with all of your prospects. More than that, *Knock Your Socks Off Prospecting: How to Cold Call, Get Qualified Leads, and Make More Money* is about creating a personal program of cold-call selling, building the skills necessary to work it, and developing the stamina—the patience—to do so, until one day you, like young Thomas, become a master of cold-call selling.

Skip Miller
Ron Zemke

Acknowledgments

Planning and preparation are the keys to almost everything, and so it was in the writing of *Knock Your Socks Off Prospecting: How to Cold Call, Get Qualified Leads, and Make More Money*. Without help from a host of characters, this last book in the "Knock Your Socks Off" series would not have been completed.

What makes this book different from all the others in the series is that during the writing of *Knock Your Socks Off Prospecting: How to Cold Call, Get Qualified Leads, and Make More Money*, Ron Zemke, whose "Socks Off" style has become familiar to so many readers, passed away after a long battle with cancer. Ron's trademark humor, insight, and "no-bull, lighten up, the problem isn't as grave as you are making it" attitude are very much present in this book, and for that I am deeply grateful.

Thanks are due first to AMACOM and Ellen Kadin, who had the idea to get Ron and me together and the patience to see this project through. Ron's style and insight, my sales expertise, both our energies—it just seemed to work.

Illustrator John Bush once again delivered above and beyond our expectations. Ron told me going into this that John's uncanny grasp of the "Socks Off" spirit had amazed him for nearly fifteen years. Now I'm amazed too. Thanks, John.

A very special thank-you to Susan Zemke, whose strength and bravery were an inspiration, and who insisted that Ron wanted this book to be finished. Chip Bell and Tom Connellan, Ron's partners and colleagues, also have been extremely supportive.

My personal thanks to Jill and Jack for helping me with the "Socks Off" writing style late in the game, when Ron was no longer able to. Yes, they had to use a sledgehammer, but they worked real hard at it.

To my family, friends, and customers, I learn from you more than I ever teach, so thanks for teaming with us to help people sell better and be happier doing it. As always, Kyle, Alexandra, and Brianna...you are the best and my inspiration.

Ron Zemke succeeded in most things that he did, and it is in his honor that all of us worked so hard to make this, hopefully, the best "Socks Off" book ever published. Or at least the best one about sales. Oh, all right, the best about prospecting.

Ron, you will be missed. But your spirit will live, thrive, and knock people's socks off for a long time to come...we promise.

Skip Miller
January 2005

Introduction:

The Art of Prospecting

Selling is fun. Or at least it should be. Winning the deal, working with people, being on the front lines and clued into what's really happening out in the field—it's fun. Selling is a great profession.

In any profession, however, there are parts of the job that people like the most and parts they like the least. In software development, the most dreaded chore is documentation. In engineering, it's detail-drawing specifications. In finance, it's the drudgery of the numbers.

The thing most salespeople like least about their profession is prospecting. In fact, many salespeople hate it. Finding new leads, cold calling, getting prospects into the sales pipeline, ramping up the sales funnel—yikes! Most salespeople know what to do with a prospect once he or she has been found and qualified, but getting and pursuing those leads …well, that's a chore they'd rather avoid.

There is a difference between salespeople who are good at prospecting—sometimes called rainmakers—and those who aren't. The difference is not something you'd suspect. It's that the ones who do it well consider prospecting an art and not a science.

When you treat prospecting scientifically, you're dealing in absolutes. There are laws to follow. There are rules you must work within to achieve a goal or acceptable outcome. There is stress and pressure to accomplish that single desired outcome so that you can move onto the next step in the sales process, with its own single acceptable outcome, and then the next step, and the next. It means you are always completely dependent on someone else for success—namely, the prospect.

When you stop pretending that prospecting is a science and instead treat it as an art—your whole perspective will change. Formal rules become guidelines and tools. Goals become multifaceted, with many different outcomes not only possible but acceptable. Prospecting becomes something that you can control, because you are the artist and this is your canvas. If you start a work of art and don't like it, you can stop what you're doing and start another one. You can begin an unlimited number of art pieces to see which ones are best suited to what you really want to do. There's no limit to how many you can begin.

The so-called science of selling is overrated, and it scares most salespeople to death—because if the steps of a scientific process are followed correctly you should achieve the predicted result every time. Whenever a sales call doesn't work out the way the scientific process says it should, the failure must lie with you. The process can't be fallible, so you must have screwed up! This isn't actually stated, of course—nobody with an ounce of sanity claims to have a system that will guarantee success with every single cold call. But if selling is a science, and most of your cold calls don't result in sales, then wow, you must be doing something really wrong.

Conversely, by treating prospecting as an art, the pressure is off. Mistakes are okay. You can develop your own style, based on some sales principles and tools that are easily mastered.

Knock Your Socks Off Prospecting: How to Cold Call, Get Qualified Leads, and Make More Money is definitely an art. We will offer suggestions and give you some quick tools to use to hone your craft. But remember, the Mona Lisa wasn't created in a day, and you aren't required to become the master of the prospecting universe overnight. Instead, your aim simply should be to get better at prospecting. Even a 10 percent improvement would make a big difference. A 20 percent improvement would be huge.

And you will get better. In fact, you're going to knock their socks off. We promise.

In Memoriam

We are greatly saddened by the loss of Ron Zemke who passed away on August 17, 2004. We worked with Ron on many books over the course of fifteen years. He was a fine author who offered much wisdom and wit to readers throughout the world, and a wonderful colleague whose mighty spirit and transcendent humor were gifts to us all.

Part One

The Fundamentals of Knock Your Socks Off Prospecting

When approaching someone who might be a candidate to become a customer of your company, you are making a cold call. The most difficult kind of cold call is when the person you approach:

- Has never heard of your company.
- Doesn't believe he or she has any use for your product or service.
- Seems to be annoyed that you are bothering him.

The best kind of cold call is when the person you approach:

- Knows your company.
- Knows something about your product or service.
- Knows that he or she has a need.

1

- Has heard about you.
- Had meant to call you.

Put gold stars on the days when you call one of those people. They are priceless and need to be cherished.

But a cold call actually is just one step—a late step—in a larger process called prospecting. Prospecting begins when we start asking questions like, "Whom should we call in the first place?" "What can we learn about these people and their needs before we make our cold calls?" "How should we approach them?" "How can we otherwise increase the chances that a cold call will be successful?"

In other words, a successful cold call is the payoff in a series of activities that add up to successful prospecting. The ultimate goal of all prospecting activities is to create and enable successful cold calls.

In Part One, we are going to discuss how you can prepare to succeed at cold calling. That means we'll talk about the larger process of prospecting—such as how to define your purpose and your prospecting goals. We'll explain the fundamentals of Knock Your Socks Off Prospecting.

There isn't a lot of preliminary work to do, but these preliminaries will have a huge impact on your success. Remember your Mom saying, "If you are going to do something, you might as well do it right?" Mom wasn't talking about prospecting, but she may as well have been. The next thirteen chapters will help prepare you for Knock Your Socks Off Prospecting.

1
Gee, Ma, Do I Have To?

No one was ever lost on a straight road.

—Indian Proverb

Most salespeople hate to prospect. They will do almost anything to avoid it. They would rather eat dirt. They would rather break a leg. They would rather see their in-laws move in next door. They would rather . . . you get the idea.

If you are a typical salesperson, this fear and loathing of prospecting is so engrained that you'll never be persuaded to love it. So we won't try. Don't worry, we won't ask you to chant, "I love prospecting, I love prospecting," instead of watching your favorite TV show.

What we will ask you to do is accept that part of your job is to prospect for leads and close those leads. No, don't say it. We have heard all the arguments:

♦ "I am a salesperson, not a lead-generation machine."
♦ "There are two types of salespeople: those who like to prospect and those who would rather focus on working current business relationships. I am one of the latter."
♦ "I'm just too busy to prospect. I have a ton of stuff to do."
♦ "Should I prospect today or poke myself in the eye with a pencil? The pain is about the same."

Sorry, but none of that will wash. You don't have to like cold calling, but you do have to do it. And because you do, why not learn to excel at it? We will venture to say that strong prospecting skills are rarer than 10-karat diamonds. Therefore, they are extremely valuable. If you have to do something anyway, and if learning to do it well increases your earning power and market value, then what the heck, let's knock some socks off!

While you don't have to love cold calling, nothing in your job description actually requires you to hate it, either, right? Maybe you'd even concede that there are some positive things to be said for cold calling. Think about it. A successful cold call is a huge adrenaline rush, isn't it? And because it's something you can never "master," you can keep learning and improving at it forever instead of growing bored. You might not believe this yet, but prospecting actually can be fun. (Don't throw that brick! Read on.)

Excelling at prospecting and cold calling is as much about dealing with your fears as it is about learning new skills. Here's a little secret: You had other opportunities to learn the mental and tactical skills required to become a great prospecting machine, but you have always stopped short because you have been heavily conditioned to hate and fear cold calling.

Fear can paralyze. A friend of ours is a little league baseball coach. He told us that at the beginning of every season about half of the kids are afraid of facing a fastball, especially one thrown by someone their own age. They can't concentrate on trying to hit the ball because they're too afraid of being hit by the ball.

The coach came up with a simple but effective solution. "Typically, a kid practices two or three times per week, and during a practice he will see twenty pitches in batting practice. So that's forty to sixty pitches per week—and most of those are from the coach, because the kids are less scared when a coach is pitching.

"What I am going to have these kids do," he said, "is face 200 to 300 pitches per week in practice, and mostly from our best pitchers, so they get used to it. The longer they do it, the more comfortable they will become and the more confidence they will have during a game. It's confidence I'm after, not just talent. You need both to get a hit."

He tried it. It worked. His team brought home the championship trophy! Sounds like he would make a great sales manager.

With practice, you will learn to laugh at your cold-calling fears. We're going to show you how to prospect so that you will be knocking your own socks off.

> **TIP:** Practice your sales prospecting speech by leaving it on your own voice mail. Then listen to what you hear. You'll be able to hear the message you are leaving for others and make changes to it so that it says exactly what you want it to say. Have some other people listen to it as well and get their feedback. Above all, practice, practice, practice.

2
Make Money Easier

Go out and buy a 5-cent pencil, a 25-cent notebook and begin to write down some million dollar ideas yourself.

—Bob Grinde

You work for a company, you sell something, and then you get rewarded for it . . . you get paid! And you can control your income level to a greater degree than in most professions, which is one of the reasons sales is an appealing career.

Below are three rules to follow in this game of selling. They'll make your job a whole lot easier and your income a whole lot higher.

- ◆ Be positive.
- ◆ Be aggressive.
- ◆ Be persistent.

Be Positive

"I hate cold calling but, Lord help me, it's a chore I have to do."

My, with that attitude, how do you think you are coming across to prospects over the phone? Oh, you have the ability to just "turn it on" when you want to? Sure you do! Just like you can flap your arms and fly to Paris.

A positive attitude is overwhelmingly important in cold calling. People want to talk to positive people. And positive, happy attitudes are contagious. The emotional undertone in the message you leave, the e-mail you send, or the conversation you have with a prospect comes across louder than the message itself.

TIP: Communication Variables

  ◆ **Content** – What is being said
  ◆ **Tonality** – How something is being said
  ◆ **Nonverbal** – Other messages that come across
      to the recipient

Some studies show that most people believe that content accounts for 40 to 60 percent of effective communication, tonality accounts for 20 to 30 percent, and nonverbal messages (eye movement, held tilt, pauses in a conversation) account for the remaining 20 to 30 percent.

In reality, content counts for about 7 percent, tonality for 38 percent, and nonverbal communication for 55 percent. That means 93 percent of communication has to do with how you say something, not what you say. Think of arguments you've had with your spouse or with a sullen teenager. It isn't what they say that drives you nuts, right? It's how they say it.

A positive attitude will win you friends, bring you rewards, and make you more successful at cold calling. Sure, it's possible to overdo it ("Hey, kids! It's Howdy Doody time!!!"), but good cheer should not be reserved for the holidays.

Be Aggressive

"Hi, I'm not here right now, but if you leave your name and number, I'll get back to you as soon as I can. If it's important, you can get me on my cell phone at 555-5555."

How many salespeople do you think call that cell phone number? How many take that simple extra step? About 9 percent. Which means that 91 percent of salespeople are saying, in effect, "What I am offering is not really that important, so I'll just leave a message."

The order goes to the salesperson who asks for it, not the one who presents a great case and waits for the buyer to say, "OK, I'll take it."

There is a fine line between aggressive and obnoxious. What's the difference? The aggressive salesperson wants to help the prospect; the obnoxious one just wants to help himself. Aggressive salespeople genuinely believe that what they have to offer will help their prospect in a big way. And that comes across every cold-calling day.

The salesperson who is aggressive does their homework, knows that what they offer can help their prospect, and is on a mission to help. The salesperson is obnoxious who just keeps trying to sell something to someone regardless of need, and who keeps score only on their wins rather than how many customers they have helped. Prospects can tell the difference in the first 30 seconds.

Be Persistent

Abraham Lincoln is regarded as one of the greatest leaders America ever had. But consider this:

- ◆ Lincoln was defeated when he ran for the Illinois House of Representatives in 1832. But he was victorious in the House race in 1834, and was then reelected for three consecutive terms.
- ◆ Lincoln was defeated when he ran for the U.S. House of Representatives in 1843, then ran successfully for a House seat in 1846.
- ◆ He was defeated for the Senate in 1855.
- ◆ He was defeated for vice president in 1856.
- ◆ He was defeated for the Senate again in 1858.
- ◆ Finally, in 1860, Lincoln was elected president.

Persistence is the ability to take a defeat without giving up—to learn from it and eventually turn it into a positive. What you do with those nonreturned e-mails and phone call is up to you. But the more persistent you are, the more successful you will be.

TIP: Persistence Opens the Buying Window

Many things have to be right to get a sale. You need to have the right product or service, right price, and you need to talk to the right people. But the *time* must be right as well, and we're talking about the buyer's time, not yours. The buying window has to be open.

Perhaps you've placed five calls to a certain prospect, and then just given up: "He never returns my calls, so there is no interest there." And meanwhile, maybe the buyer was saying, "You know, I'm buried this week, but next week I really must get back to that salesperson." Next week, the "buying window" is open and the prospect will take your call—if you are persistent enough to make it. It's often simple persistence that puts you in the right place at the right time.

Positive, aggressive, and persistent—remember those three guidelines. You'll make more money, your job will get easier, and you may even learn to enjoy cold calling a heck of a lot more. Hey, we all like things that are easy and successful, don't we?

3

It's All About Them

That's enough about me . . . what do you think of me?

—Bette Midler in "Beaches"

You have just come back from vacation. It was a great trip, and you captured the highlights in some terrific photos. You want to show the pictures to Phil, your neighbor. You're sure he'd love to see them. Not all 322 of them, of course, but certainly the twelve best ones. You race over to Phil's house and whip them out.

It takes maybe three minutes to show Phil your best shots, with running commentary. When you're done, what does Phil say? Does he say: "Hey, that looks like it was a great trip. Tell me more." Or maybe: "These are stunning. Have you ever thought of getting into professional photography?"

No, he doesn't. In the real world, what Phil says is: "Hey, these are great. Want to see some of the pictures I took of my kid's birthday party last week?"

This is Phil. Your buddy. Someone who actually does care about you and what you've been up to. And still, three minutes about you and your doings was his limit.

Now suppose that instead of talking to your pal Phil, you're talking to a prospect who is a complete stranger. No matter how marvelous the photos in your brochure may be, what do you suppose that prospect's limit is for listening to you talk about *you*?

In sales, and especially in cold calling, it's all about THEM. It's never about you. Prospects don't care about you, and they don't care much about your company, either. Prospects care about their own worlds, their own lives, their

11

problems, their issues, and the fires they're trying to put out right now. That's what they want to talk about. And that's what they *will* talk to you about—if you give them a reason to talk to you at all.

Put First Things First

Customers buy from salespeople they like and trust. The question becomes, how do you get prospects to like and trust you? The best way to build rapport quickly is to let them talk about things that are important to them while you listen attentively. So put first things first. What is important to prospects?

◆ Whatever their boss says is important
◆ Whatever they are currently working on
◆ Whatever they're working weekends to keep up with
◆ What they really like to do
◆ What makes them the most mone
◆ What makes them look good to their boss
◆ What gets them promoted
◆ What gets them home at an earlier hour
◆ What gets them excited
◆ What gets rid of their current headache
◆ What gets the biggest pain-in-the-neck person in their company off their back

Please notice that a few things *you* find fascinating are conspicuously absent from that list:

♦ Your product or service
♦ Your company, its activities, and its grandeur
♦ Your desire to sell something
♦ You

Put like that, very few salespeople would argue with it. But when cold calling, how many salespeople waste most or all of the precious time available for establishing rapport by yakking about the things on the prospect's "don't care" list? Yes, you may have to take 10 or 20 seconds of a cold call (or a letter, or an e-mail) to let the prospect know who you are, but after that, it has to be all about them.

The Us to Them Ratio

In a typical cold call, voicemail message, or prospecting letter, how much time should you spend talking about them and how much should you spend talking about you? The ratio needs to vary a bit depending on the situation, but the ideal ratio is 90:10—90 percent about them and 10 percent about you.

In some of the best sales calls you ever made, all you said was, "Yes, we can do that." In the worst ones, you went on a talking spree, and the prospect fell asleep. When the conversation is about them, they are energized and involved. When it's about you, you are energized and involved. Which is more important? (Hint: They're the ones deciding whether to spend the money.)

If a 90:10 ratio in favor of the prospect is simply unachievable in your situation, at least try for 70:30. After a good introduction, short and to the point, most of the conversation, the letter, or the e-mail had better be about them.

TIP: Record yourself delivering the standard opening speech you use to begin a cold call or to leave a voicemail message. Then listen to how many times you use the word "I." The more you use it, the more the focus of your message is on you. Try for no "I's," and watch your success rate soar.

What About Your Support Material?

Take a look at your marketing brochures, your PowerPoint presentations, and the marching orders you got from your boss. Chances are, they're all about your company, your products, you, you, you. Time to change that, to whatever extent you can.

Lobby your marketing department to create support material focused on the things that prospects care about. Design your own letters and sales pitches to center on their concerns, not yours. Use support material that gets prospects to think about themselves, what they are doing, and how they might be doing it differently. Use material that prompts them to ask questions so you have a place to start talking.

The goal behind everything you do should be to have them pull out *their* vacation pictures, not ask to see yours again. That won't be happening anytime soon.

We will have a lot more to say about this in Part Two, and we'll describe a number of tools and techniques you can use to encourage them to drag out their photos. Until then, just remember: In prospecting, everything, always, is all about them.

4

Turn Strangers into Customers

There is no such thing as chance.

—Henry Ford

Picking up the phone to call a list of total strangers or going around knocking on doors is a brutal way to make a living. That is pure, unadulterated cold calling. Many salespeople do it, and in some situations it really is the only option.

For most salespeople however, there are strategies available that tremendously improve the odds of success by giving you targets that are easier to hit. We have found the three most useful strategies are:

- ♦ Cold to warm
- ♦ Shotguns and rifles
- ♦ Leverage

Cold to Warm

Warm calls work better than cold calls. In a cold call, you are a perfect stranger contacting a prospect out of the blue. In a warm call, the prospect has some sense of familiarity with you and will be more open to a discussion. Your objective, then, is not to make as many cold calls as you can, but to turn as many cold calls as you can into warm ones, thereby increasing your chances for success before you pick up the phone or knock on the door.

How to turn a call from cold to warm? There are several ways:

◆ Reference someone inside the prospective company.
◆ Reference someone outside the prospective company.
◆ Reference common customers.
◆ Refer to a flattering story in a newspaper or magazine about your company or the prospect's company.
◆ Ask prospects to attend an event they would find interesting and worth their time.

Any time you can move your approach from cold to warm before making the call or requesting the appointment, your chance for success improves.

Warm Calls in Action

"How does she do it?" one salesperson asked another. When leads came in the door right after a trade show, this company's sales reps would call the people who stopped by the booth to request more information. Their success rate was low: They were able to reach the prospects or get them to return messages less than 10 percent of the time. "Guess they were just window shoppers," the salespeople surmised.

Judy, however, was getting people to call her back at an astonishing rate of 30 to 40 percent. "My secret is to call the boss," she explained. " Bosses are the ones who approved expenses for these prospects to travel to the show. If they sent their people to the show, they must have perceived some need. So why not ask bosses why they spent the money?"

Judy has two additional reasons she likes to talk to the boss first:

1. "It's harder to go up the organization than down."

2. "Whether I reach the boss or not, when I call the show attendee I always mention that I have spoken with or left a message for the boss. That gets their attention."

Judy's "secret" was no secret at all. She just turned cold calls into warm ones.

Shotguns and Rifles

A shotgun spreads a broad pattern, but even so, you still have to aim. You don't just walk outdoors and start blasting into the sky, hoping to hit a duck. You have to pick a lake, a field, or some other place where you think the ducks are. Then you have to point the gun in the direction of the ducks before you pull the trigger. The same strategy applies in prospecting. Even when you're using a shotgun you must be both broad and specific. If you want to hit a prospect, go where good prospects are most likely to be before you start shooting.

Use the shotgun approach to target a broad market. It could be a vertical market, like the automotive industry. It could be a geographic market, like the city of Phoenix, or it could be customer-oriented, as in "past customers who have bought Product X from us before."

Rifle techniques allow you to refine your approach and become more productive. Here are three of them:

1. **Create goals**. "How many by when?" is the key here. All of your prospecting goals should include the specific numbers of contacts you will make and when you will make them. Goals that use words like "soon" or "a lot" will probably not be met, because "soon" is not a date in your calendar. Write the goals down. Studies show that a written goal is three times more likely to be obtained than a goal that is not in writing.

2. **Be timely**. Work to the prospect's time frame, not yours. The best times to reach prospects are early in the morning, in the evening, ten minutes before the hour, and ten minutes before and after the lunch hour.

3. **Create influence**. Turning cold calls into warm calls has already been discussed, but think "rifle" by warming up your calls as specifically as you can. This will require additional homework, but for a major prospect it is worth the effort. Do you know somebody who also knows the prospect and will let you use him as a reference? If you do some research, can you find that newspaper article about the prospect's company instead of just happening to see it? Is there someone in your company who has specific contacts or information that you can use to get through to a top prospect?

Leverage

You can gain leverage by adopting one of the following three tactics.

♦ **The Expert.** If you are an expert in your field, say so. If there is any way you can position yourself or your company as having some special expertise, do it, do it, do it.

■ "I am the leading real estate salesperson in the city."
■ "I have been in this industry for twenty five years."
■ "My company is the #1 supplier in the world for form brackets."

- "We have forty-six out of the top one hundred medical device companies as customers."
- "I have been ranked #1 by the XYZ organization in providing assistance and services to the food and beverage industry."

TIP: Find Your Expertise

How can you or your company leverage your knowledge or capabilities into expert status? Here are a few examples from this book's authors.

As of this writing, Skip Miller's book *ProActive Sales Management* is ranked # 1 out of more than 60,000 books in Amazon.com's sales category. Skip doesn't know and doesn't care where Barnes and Noble or anyone else ranks it; because Amazon says it's # 1, he ends up being an expert.

One of Ron Zemke's books, *Delivering Knock Your Socks Off Service*, has sold more than 750,000 copies. That number alone makes him an expert.

♦ **The Question.** What are the one or two burning questions for which your top customers need answers? What is really bugging them? What is happening in their day-to-day life that you can assist with?

- "What are you doing to take advantage of the current interest rates?"
- "Eight out of ten people in your position ask us, 'Why is this the time to invest in capital equipment?'"
- "What is happening for the holiday season, and how can you capitalize on it?"

These are ways to catch buyers' attention and generate interest in what you have to say or why you are calling them. If they have no interest in a well-crafted question or two, the buying window may be closed right now, and you should try again in a few weeks or months. If your questions are valid, it will be only a matter of time before the need that your question brings up arises.

◆ **The Value Statement.** A value statement tells buyers that by taking action, they can get some value over and above their expectations.

■ Many people have asked for this, and we have now packaged it so you can get the most popular features immediately and at no additional charge.

■ It now offers twice as many cycles as previous models.

■ Because of demand, you now can get this at the lowest price in the industry. The thing to remember is that the value you offer must be special in the *buyer's* mind, not just in yours. Your new model may be a marvel of engineering, but if the buyer doesn't care how many cycles it has, you need another value statement. What kinds of things do buyers value?

■ How can I get more for the same money?

■ Can I can get it without waiting?

■ What do I have to do to get this installed without a lot of risk and effort?

To understand value, you must think like a buyer, not like someone who would just like to make a sale.

5

The Ol' Numbers Game

The King is the man who can.

—Thomas Carlyle

Cold calling is a numbers game. Now there's something new, eh? But some numbers are more significant than others. Yes, the number of total calls you make and total appointments committed to are important, but there are some other key numbers that require special attention if you want to be a Knock Your Socks Off prospector.

The Numbers in Action

"Investing in real estate can become very confusing-there are so many things to consider when buying a house," says our friend Jon, a savvy real estate agent. "You've got curb appeal, square footage, the age of the house, the number of schools and amenities nearby -not to mention the number of bathrooms, amount of cabinet space, and the brand of appliances—it becomes overwhelming."

Jon's life got a lot simpler and he became more successful when he figured out that some numbers are more important than others in his line of work.

> "Now I focus on the size of the lot, the size of the kitchen, and comparables in the area," he says. "That's all I really pay attention to. If those numbers are working for me, I invest, and I usually come out ahead. When those numbers are not as good as I'd like, and I still make an investment, I usually do not do as well as I'd hoped."

Following is a discussion of the numbers and measurements that count most for successful prospectors. Keep a running tab on which one you use in your success so you can tell you are getting better.

Total Calls or E-Mails Connected

This is a ratio of the number of attempts made to the number of the actual contacts made . . . If you cold-called or e-mailed one hundred prospects in a day, and ten people either e-mailed or called you back, your ratio would be 10 percent. Typical ratios in this area are 2 to 3 percent. If all you do is work hard at the cold-to-warm suggestions discussed in Chapter 4, your ratio should increase to around 5 or 7 percent. If you're able to incorporate all of the tools in this book, your ratio should rise to 11 to 17 percent.

The time frame for counting valid responses is forty eight to seventy two hours. (Choose what makes sense in your situation, but remember that the shorter the time frame, the quicker you can take additional action.) If you have not heard back in forty eight to seventy two hours, record the cold call as a nonconnect.

Talk Time

Talk time is a very effective measurement if you are doing a lot of phone work. The measure is simply: How long did you have the prospect on the phone? There is a direct correlation between time on the phone (on a per call basis) and success. A

typical cold-call sale will have a talk time of one to three minutes. A really good cold call will have a talk time of three to
seven minutes. Great calls for a high-dollar sale can last for
twenty or thirty minutes.

Find out what the average talk time is in your business,
because the ideal talk time varies depending on what you sell.
When you learn the average, triple it. That will be your new
goal. You'll be amazed at how easy it is to reach.

> **TIP:** There are computer programs that can track
> talk time if you use them to dial out. Additionally, if
> you use VoIP, you can add a feature to your ser-
> vice that will keep track by number called.

Next Step Calls

Of the total cold calls in which you made contact, how many
prospects agreed to take a next step within a specific time
frame? For instance, how many agreed to meet with you at 8
A.M. next Tuesday? ("Sometime after the holidays, maybe,"
doesn't count.)

Measure next step successes for first calls only. Once you
have the prospect in a process, you're not cold calling anymore. The following are all that need to be tracked to measure
your cold calls:

- ◆ If you had a conversation with them
- ◆ If you got them to agree to a next step by a certain time
- ◆ If they actually met the commitment

Aim for a success rate of 60 to 70 percent.

Management Contacts Made

This one applies to business-to-business sales. It's the same as "total calls connected," but it applies to contact with the senior managers of the company you're targeting—the people most likely to make final buying decisions.

We knew a salesperson who had a goal of collecting off-white business cards. He wanted to get one hundred off-white business cards per year. Why? Well, it seems that at his biggest account, only managers had off-white business cards. He wanted to make sure he was calling at the senior levels as often as possible. "Without a goal, how would I know if I was being successful?" he explained.

Reference Calls

What percent of the cold calls you make are actually warm in some way instead of purely cold? Again, this varies by industry and type of selling. And regardless of your industry, this metric is a bit tricky. Cold calls that are too high in the cold area obviously will hinder your success, but in most selling situations too many warm calls also should be a warning sign. Why? It probably means you're doing so much homework that you aren't making enough calls. This is still a numbers game, remember?

Keep your goals flexible in order to stay sharp. If you are not making enough calls, lower your target for the percentage that should be warm. If too few prospects are returning your calls, raise your warm-call target and start doing more homework before you call.

Of course we all hate to keep track of what we do. And yes, "just go out and do it" is often a good rule in sales. But unless you pay attention to these numbers, you are going to spin your wheels a heck of a lot to get results you could achieve with far less time and effort. Keep track of the five measurements discussed in this chapter, and you will see the difference in your pocketbook.

6

A Winning Formula

It's what you do with what you've got.

—Leroy Van Dyke

How do you determine whether you're a successful salesperson? What measures do you use? There is your quota—what you need to achieve to be successful. Then there is your earnings goal—what you expect to earn in order to achieve the lifestyle you want.

If you think about it, however, those are reactive measures. Hitting your quotas and meeting your earning goals are *results* you obtain because you have certain skills and you took certain actions. The question is, how do you set about achieving those results? If you want to get ahead of the curve in prospecting—or sales in general—take a look at some proactive measures.

- ◆ **Reactive** goals and measures are ones that result from your actions.
- ◆ **Proactive** measures are ones that tell you which actions to take.

The Proactive Equation

Success in prospecting will come when you master enough *skills* to be proficient, and you perform a lot of the right *activ-*

ities that will yield the results you want. Skills and activities are the key factors. The formula is:

$$\$ = S \times A^2$$
$$\$uccess = Skills \times Activities^2$$

Success results from the **S**kills you have multiplied by the amount of cold-calling **A**ctivities you perform, squared. Yes, we're telling you that **A**ctivities are geometrically more important than **S**kills. The successful Knock Your Socks Off salesperson focuses on both. As we proceed, that formula will be our guide.

Skills

We'll talk about skills at length in later chapters. For now, allow us to suggest that you try to improve one skill a week. Really work on it. It could be anything. Here are a few suggestions to get your started:

- ◆ Opening speech
- ◆ Closing speech
- ◆ Homework skills
- ◆ Communication skills
- ◆ Time management skills
- ◆ Negotiation skills
- ◆ Phone skills
- ◆ Writing skills
- ◆ Computer skills

Pick one of the skills we call "tools" in this book. Pick a skill from a training program you've attended. But every week, choose something to get better at and make a real attempt to improve. Spend up to twenty minutes a day focusing specifically on developing and improving this one skill. The main idea is simply to keep yourself sharp. Do you really want to sell to today's prospects using skills you haven't honed in years?

Activities

So much to do, so little time. And hey, you've been bitten before, putting a lot of effort into activities that sounded important but ended up being a waste of time. Why bother? What's the point? Where do you begin? Where do you focus? Here's a hint:

> **FOCUS ON ACTIVITIES THAT WILL PRODUCE THE RESULTS YOU WANT WITHIN THE NEXT NINETY DAYS.**

Start with an assessment: Given your territory, the status of your accounts, the number of accounts you have, the kind of accounts they are, etc., what activities need to get done over the next ninety days that will really make a difference? This is just a wild hunch, but perhaps you fall into one of the categories that follow. If so, our recommendations might help.

The Low Caller

Take a look at your current sales forecast. If 50 percent or more of your "real-close-to-closing" prospects are people who aren't very near the top of the buying organization's totem pole, you have a problem. Middle managers won't cut it. For you to get a good-size deal, a vice president, president, or owner will need to be in the picture. If you have at least met this senior level person, good for you; you have them involved. Now get them committed.

The difference between involved and committed is the difference between ham and eggs. The chicken is involved, the pig is committed.

The Too Few

Way too often we believe ourselves when we say we are too busy to prospect. "I just need to close these two more deals, and then I'll have time to do a really good job at prospecting." The time to make cold calls is when you have too few prospects, not when you have none. There are twenty four hours in a day. Find one of those hours and devote it to prospecting.

The Too Many

This is the opposite of the Too Few: You have a lot of prospects but no time to focus on turning any of them into buyers. The solution is to pick no more than three and dedicate 60 to 80 percent of your time to those three. The rest will move along, and some will actually heat up, causing you to cheat and try to balance four or five. That's fine, except that it can lead you right back to twenty five. Most salespeople can really only balance three to five major sales at one time. Try three for now to get into a groove. It is a discipline, but one that will keep you focused on what is important.

The Deep but Not Wide

You have some good corporate accounts, but you have not taken the time to prospect into other divisions or departments of these accounts. Either that or you are selling only one product line when you could be selling more. You're deep but not wide. Again, set a goal that you will contact X number of people within a specific time frame. A situation like this is leaving money on the table. That's no way to knock anybody's socks off.

Here's a quick and easy way to increase your contact visibility. We call it the "Make a Friend a Week" rule. Talk to one of your existing customers once a week, and dig deep for possible contacts within the organization. This will enable you to go both deep and wide within your existing client organizations.

A Case of the *Maybes*

Yes's are great, *no's* are disappointing . . . but *maybe's* will kill you. If you're working on ten deals right now, and you close eight, congratulations, you have done well. If you're working ten deals and you lose eight, that's too bad, but you know you are doing something wrong and you can fix it. If you're working ten deals and you have eight *maybe's*, do you figure that's OK because you still have a chance? You may want to reconsider.

Maybe's will sit in your sales forecast, and sit there, and sit there, and slip, slip, slip, and all you can do is "wait for something to happen."

Acts of God aside, there is something more proactive you can do to deal with *maybe's.* Ask the prospect for their implementation date.

 ## The Implementation Date (I-Date)

The implementation date (I-Date) is not the date when clients say they'll buy from you—that's something only you care about. The I-Date is the date when clients intend to use your product or put it into service—and that's what they care about. Think about it: Does it matter to you when you bought your vacation package or do you just care when you're going on vacation?

Does it matter when you bought the anniversary gift, or when you give it? Look in your current sales forecast. Do you have real I-Dates for your "maybe" prospects? If you do, great. If not, ask them. When do they plan to use the thing you are selling?

If you're an average salesperson, 30 to 40 percent of what you're working on is *maybe's*. It's time to get rid of those and focus on real prospects who need your attention.

Hone your skills, build a ninety-day activity list, and clean up the *maybe's*. You will increase your prospecting success more than you ever thought possible.

7

Time Management I:

The ProActive Sales Matrix™

Don't serve time, make time serve you.

—Willie Sutton

I have too much to do, and it all needs to get done. It gets to a point where I don't have time to go to the bathroom. And you're telling me to make more time for prospecting?

Salespeople are so busy that prospecting becomes just one more thing sliding toward the bottom of the to-do list. You know you should do it, and you will—someday, when you have the time.

Of course, this won't do. In this chapter and the next, we will describe two tools that will help you manage your time better. The ProActive Sales Matrix™ will is presented in this chapter and the PowerHour is presented in Chapter 8.

To introduce the first of these tools, let's start with a story.

"How can I spend my time more wisely?" asked the young student to the wise sage.

"Silly boy," answered the sage. "Have you not learned the way of the great hunter?

"No, wise one, please tell me."

"An ordinary hunter goes into the woods to hunt game for his family. With geese, ducks and pheasant relatively abundant, the hunter knows there is food out there. With a lot of work, he gets some food every day. The hunting is long, but he comes home with a bird so his family does not starve."

"This is wise, is it not?" asked the youth.

"It isn't stupid," the sage conceded. "But the ordinary hunter must hunt from sunup to sundown just to kill enough birds to feed his family for a day. The great hunter is different, however. The great hunter hunts birds, but he also spends some time hunting buffalo. If he kills a buffalo, his family can eat for a month."

"It seems the great hunter is wiser, but also that he works much harder than the ordinary hunter," the boy observed.

"This is not so young one," said the sage. "On days when he finds no buffalo, it is true the great hunter can take a little longer to get his birds. But when he does find a buffalo, he gets a month's worth of food for a day's worth of effort."

Did you ever notice it often takes the same amount of effort to close a $100,000 order as it does to close a $5,000 order? But you get used to hunting birds, you know where the birds hang out, and quite frankly, you like hunting birds. Bird hunting winds up consuming so much of your day that you have no time to hunt buffalo. So you tell yourself there are no buffalo in your territory. Everyone else's territory has buffalo, but yours is strictly for the birds.

It's true that selling to buffalo is different from selling to birds. But we're talking about cold calling here, and how to make time to do it.

The ProActive Sales Matrix™

The ProActive Sales Matrix™ will give you a clearer understanding of the way you are spending your time today and make it far more obvious how you can find time to prospect among the buffalos. Let's start with a typical sales forecast time management scale that ranks prospects as A, B, or C. This is the way a salesperson usually forecasts:

- ◆ **A = Current Hot Prospects.** These are accounts you're banking on. A 90 percent factor is typically assigned to these prospects, meaning that the salesperson is 90% sure the deal will come in.
- ◆ **B = Medium Prospects.** These are works in progress, somewhere in the sales funnel. A 60 to 70 percent factor usually is assigned to them.
- ◆ **C = Lukewarm Prospects.** More than likely these prospects have just been identified, they are just starting the sales cycle, or they are "hope and a prayer" prospects. These accounts usually get a factor of 10 to 40 percent.

Now these weighted averages are okay, but there is a lot more information you can use than just a weighted guess. To turn that forecast into a far more effective time management tool, let's change the meaning of the letters a bit and add a second dimension to the A, B, C ratings. The first dimension will represent history—what the prospect has done in the past with you or your competition. The second dimension will represent the potential for future activity on the account. To keep things specific and realistic, let's limit the projections of future activity to the next 90 to 120 days.

A = Sales greater than $100,000.
B = Sales between $30,000 and $100,000.
C = Sales less than $30,000.

   Thus, instead of an A prospect, we might have an AA
prospect. The first "A" refers to past activity on the account,
the second to projected future activity during the next 90 to
120 days. (Figure 7-1.)

Figure 7-1. The ProActive Sales Matrix™.

   So, an AA account is one that has spent more than
$100,000 with you in the past or has already agreed to do so
currently (first "A"), and has the potential in the next 90 to 120
days to spend more than $100,000 with you again (second
"A"). If we assign BC status to a prospect, that means the account currently or in the past has spent between $30,000 and
$100,000 with you and has the potential in the next 90 to 120
days to spend less than $30,000.
   Now we know two valuable things: *why* it is worthwhile
to devote some time to prospecting, and *where* we should be
spending most of that time. We have identified our buffalo.
Obviously, we need to provide for the care and feeding of the
major accounts we've already got. But for prospecting pur-
poses, we don't care about the first letter in a prospect's status
equation. The buffalo are the ones with an A or B as the *second* letter (Figure 7-2.)

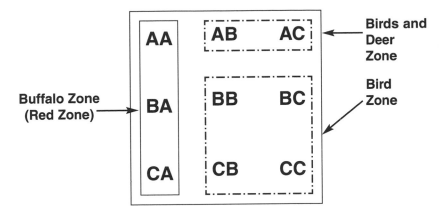

Figure 7-2. The Buffalo Zone.

You Only Get What You Hunt For

At the risk of beating this metaphor to death, you'll never get a shot at a buffalo if you're sitting in a duck blind. Salespeople miss great prospecting opportunities every day simply because it's so easy to develop habits that keep them focused on the wrong hunting territory, and therefore looking in the wrong direction.

The Bird Zone

This is where salespeople typically spend 50 to 70 percent of their time shooting ducks, geese, and the like. It should be 10 to 25 percent. The Bird Zone (also called the Dead Zone) is filled with customers calling in with problems or questions, with very little potential for additional business in the near future. The 80/20 rule applies here: Approximately 80 percent of your customers generate 20 percent of your revenue—and 80 percent of your problems! There are actually some customers in this zone whom you wish would go away and give their business to the competition.

The Bird and Deer Zone

Also called the Comfort Zone. Here we find the customers we consider most important. They are the bread and butter of our territory. They have spent a lot of money with us in the past. At the current time, however, their budgets or buying windows do not justify a great deal of our prospecting time. Yes, there is business to be had, but in the short term (the next 90 to 120 days), we can find better uses for our precious prospecting time and resources.

The Buffalo Zone

This is the Red Zone. Those big, hairy critters munching grass are prospects that have the potential to spend a lot of money with us. If we want that money, we need to invest some prospecting time. So here is where we do most of our home-work and invest most of our prospecting energy. Red Zone accounts should be clearly identified, and 10 to 30 percent of our *total* time should be proactively spent here. Concentrate especially on accounts at the BA and CA level or on trying to move accounts into a BA or CA status. Why? Because you already know the AA accounts. Chances are it's the BA and CA prospects that are crying out for more of your time, effort, and hunting skills.

Here is an example of how a salesperson might use the Matrix:

> *Susan looks at her account base to figure out how she can allocate her prospecting time proactively. She determines that an A account should be one where the revenue is $100,000 or above. B accounts are from $50,000 to $100,000, and C accounts are from $10,000 to- $50,000. Any accounts below $10,000 she keeps off the forecast.*

She decides that her second digit, time, will apply to a sixty-day window.

By using the ProActive Sales Matrix™, Susan determines where she needs to spend her time as well where she should go to hunt some buffalo. She's all through working weekends just to feed the birds.

Do you spend way too much time feeding your birds? Including some you wish would just fly away? Now you know what you can stop doing to make more time for high-potential prospecting. Be proactive. Monitor yourself for the next thirty days to make sure you spend at least 20 percent of your time in the Red Zone and less than 50 percent in the Dead Zone. Look forward, not backward.

The ProActive Sales Matrix™ gives you an objective view of what you are doing now and what you need to do to be successful in the future. It gives you a clear map of the road that leads to where your very own buffalo roam.

8

Time Management II:

The PowerHour™

Plan your work for today and every day, then work your plan.

—Norman Vincent Peale

What's the first thing you do every business morning?

Here's our guess: You look at your e-mail, check your voicemail, get yourself organized . . . and by the time you look at the clock, it's 11:00 A.M., and you wonder where your morning went. Maybe your New Year's resolution was to get hold of your time and use it, as opposed to it using you. And maybe you've made the same vow every New Year since 1985.

Your prospecting efforts will become far more effective if you turn prospecting into a regular behavior, and not a "whenever you have time" type of activity. How can you do that? Welcome to PowerHour™.

 PowerHour™

A PowerHour™ is one hour a day, five hours a week, that you set aside to focus on a particular activity—in this case, prospecting. The activity thus becomes a normal part of your day rather than something you'll get around to when you aren't so busy. Tragic truth: The day will never come when you aren't busy.

> **TIP:** Treat PowerHour™ like a workout in the morning, and reward yourself for completing it. Order that special cup of coffee. Treat yourself to something you enjoy. Make a deal with yourself that if you complete five honest PowerHours™ in a week, you'll go to the mall and buy that whoopee cushion you've had your eye on. Devise a reward structure that works for you, and do yourself a favor. You'll have earned it.

There are three types of PowerHours™:

1. For the occasional prospector
2. For the medium prospector
3. For the heavy prospector

The Occasional Prospector

PowerHour™ for the occasional prospector is a great tool. You will be able to do all of your account homework and cold calling within the five hours a week time frame. Typically, you should start by devoting 50 percent of those five hours to homework and 50 percent to cold calling. The more you prospect, the less time you should need to spend doing homework, so your ratio will rise to something like 70 to 30 percent in favor of cold calling.

The Medium Prospector

The medium prospector may require two PowerHours™ per day. Devote one hour to homework and one to cold calling (or spend half of each PowerHour™ on each of those two activities). Whatever schedule you devise, stick to it. Try like crazy not to break the routine you set up for yourself.

The Heavy Prospector

If your sales situation demands that you spend a majority of your time prospecting, try to do your "homework" Power-Hours™, in short, fifteen- to thirty-minute segments. This gives you time to get into a groove when you are cold calling, then do homework when you need a break. We think you'll find that you'll be more productive that way. This should be a daily behavior, not just something you practice every so often.

Don't forget those game animals we talked about in the Chapter 7. Focus on the Red Zone—the Buffalo Zone—during your PowerHour™ times. That's where you'll find the best returns on your time investment. Before you know it, you'll be able to buy yourself ten whoopee cushions

9

Speak the Customer's Language

England and America are two great countries separated by a common language.

—Winston Churchill

When salespeople say they hate cold calling, most of them don't mean the whole process of it. What they truly hate and fear is the first minute of the call. Does this sound familiar?

> *It isn't prospecting that I have so much trouble with. It's that first sixty seconds of a cold call. If I can get a prospect's attention, I can build rapport from there, and I'm all right. But getting their attention is a killer. How do I leave a brief voicemail that actually gets the prospect to return my call? How do I open a face-to-face conversation that the prospect is willing to continue? That's where it all falls apart for me. The wheels come off before I can get the train moving.*

In business-to-business sales, the most common solution to the "first sixty-seconds" problem lies in the fact that customers in any organization speak three distinctly different languages—and you're probably speaking the wrong language to the prospects you are calling.

The language of first-level managers and specialists is not the same as the one spoken by vice presidents (VPs). And VP lingo differs in turn from the language of CEOs and other senior executives. The difference in these tongues is that their whole basis rests on different values. That makes the disparities hugely significant. The languages wind up being as different as Spanish, Greek, and Russian.

> **TIP:** : Know the prospect's rank in the company before you call. Then speak in the native tongue of that rank.

Here are the three languages that business customers speak.

Level 1: Feature/Function

At the first level are the prospects whom salespeople call on most often. They typically have job titles such as:

- Manager
- Manufacturing Manager
- Engineering Manager
- Engineer
- Marketing Manager
- Purchasing Agent
- Director
- IT Manager
- Office Manager
- Buyer

These are users, professionals, and lower-level managers in charge of specific business operations. They speak the language of feature/function (Figure 9-1). It is based on their value system—the things they care about. Things like the following:

- Does your solution come with training?
- Does the system have the latest features on it?

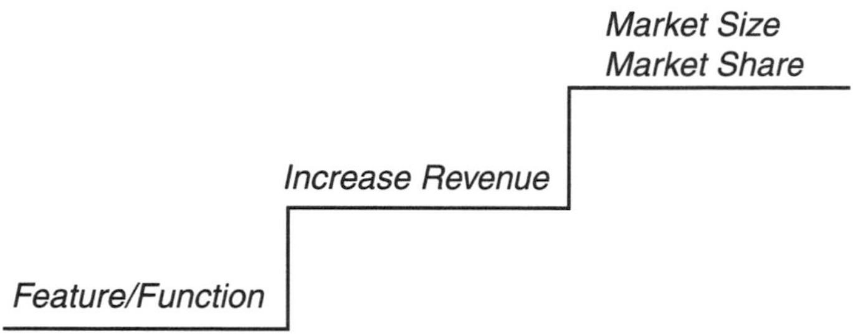

Figure 9-1. Customer languages.

♦ Can I get expedited delivery?
♦ How does this compare with last year's model?
♦ Where can I see one working?

Feature/function language is very important. Salespeople must be able to speak it fluently. That's why salespeople attend products-and-services training sessions ad nauseum—to make sure they don't look like idiots when they are unable to answer customers' questions at this level.

In the language of feature/function, customer values have to do with:

♦ Features
♦ Feature/benefit statements
♦ Feature/advantage/benefit statements
♦ Competitive features
♦ Unique features that no other provider can match

To get the serious attention of a feature/function speaker in the first sixty seconds or to leave a compelling voicemail message, you need to say things like this:

♦ "Our product can do the job 20 percent faster than your current way of doing things."
♦ "Using this new feature on the GL-3000 will lower your risk associated with testing and integration."
♦ "By using our HHR, HHL, and PTSD modules, you will be able to design those parts to more precise specifications much faster than ever before."

Feature/function is the most common language of the sales world. Salespeople are embarrassed when they can't speak it well, so it's the language in which they usually ask for marketing help. And it's the language in which they get most of that help.

Level 2: Cost/Revenue/Value

There is a huge push nowadays to "call high." Every sales guru on earth will tell you to call on higher-level decision makers in the target organization. But calling high is not the trick—anybody can leave a message for an executive. The trick is, when you call high in an organization, what do you say to persuade the exec that you are a value-add and not just a salesperson trying to peddle something?

The best feature/function statement in the world will not get you a return call from a vice president. If you have learned that painful lesson, but you don't know why, here's the reason: Vice presidents speak another language altogether (Figure 9-1).

Try to hold a feature/function conversation with a vice president, and this is what you'll hear:

> *So, you are 20 percent faster than XYZ? I didn't know that. And you're 30 percent smaller that previous models? How very interesting. Oh, and you're X.556.75Z compatible, as well? My, my. Well, that's fascinating. Thanks for coming, really. BUT . . .*
>
> *If you can't make me money or save me money, why am I talking to you?*

Vice presidents are interested in one thing only. How are you going to increase their revenue or decrease their cost? That's it! That's the value system on which their language is based. A vice president is chartered to achieve corporate goals. Corporate goals are always stated in fiscal terms: earnings, earnings before insurance and taxes (EBIT), net present value of investments (NPV), revenue per employee, compound annual growth rate (CAGR), and other fiduciary measurements. Vice presidents are responsible for the health of the business. Along with that mandate comes the responsibility that all major decisions that affect their organization be fiscally sound.

The point is not that Level 1 managers (feature/function speakers) don't care about making or saving money. They do. The point is, rather, that Level 2 managers care about nothing else. If you want to get the attention of a vice president or get your phone calls returned, some of the first words out of your mouth need to sound like this:

♦ "I'd like to talk to you about a system that has cut inventory costs in organizations like yours by 20 percent."

♦ "Our XYZ approach can boost your revenue by 10 percent, realistically, before the end of this fiscal year."

TIP: To get the attention of a buffalo prospect, speak Value language, not Feature/Function language.

Level 3: Market Size and Share

The third language companies speak is reserved for the top or senior management: presidents, CEOs, senior vice presidents, executive vice presidents, CFOs, CIOs, and so on (Figure 9-1).

The value system that shapes and forms senior management's language is based on two things: market share and market size. That's about it. How big is the market, how big can it get, and how big a share can I get? In other words, how much sand is in the sandbox, and how much of it can I either grab or hold on to?

Why Values Differ—and Why It Matters

Every year, and often every quarter, Level 3 managers must go to their bosses—shareholders, the board of directors, or maybe the private owners—to report on the state of the business as well as current and future plans. CEOs cannot address their bosses as follows:

> *"The market is growing at 14 percent CAGR over the next three years. If you adopt and approve my plans, we will grow the business by 3 percent over the next three years."*

A CEO who said that would soon be out of a job. What the CEO needs to say instead is:

> *"The market is growing at 14 percent CAGR over the next three years. If you adopt and approve my plans, we will profitably grow the business by 19 percent over the next three years and take significant share away from our competitors."*

That's how the CEO keeps his job and gets funded for another year.

The CEO then goes to the Level 2 managers (the VPs), gives them budgets for the fiscal year, and tells them to manage to those budgets—or, better, to come in under them. The CEO says things like: "I want you to deliver 10 percent more top line (revenue) while holding bottom line (costs) to budget."

Now that Level 2 managers have budgets, they formulate, re-examine, plot, manipulate, devise, and assign these budgets to different departments in their organization. How do budgets get allocated? Well, which Level 1 manager, who works for the Level 2 manager, has the best ideas that are going to increase revenue? The department that has the best ideas to help the vice president hit business goals will get the biggest share of available resources for the year. Level 1 managers who can cut costs after receiving their budgets also become heroes.

> **TIP:** : The best time to talk to Level 1 managers about how your product can **increase revenue** is **before** they have received their annual budget appropriations. The best time to talk to Level 1 man-

agers about how your product can help them **cut costs** is **after** they have received their budget appropriations. Think about it: Don't you want the biggest budget you can get before you have to worry about how to come in under it? Level 1 managers don't get bigger budgets by telling VPs they can cut costs and make do with less money. They get bigger budgets by telling VPs how they're going to generate wads of new cash. Then, if they cut costs to boot, they look like stars.

Again, the language salespeople speak most often and most fluently is Level 1 lingo—the language of feature/function. If you want to hunt buffalo, however, you need to become multilingual. Which of these languages will be the most productive for the Knock Your Socks Off prospector to know? The answer is Level 2 language—the tongue of vice presidents. When you're prospecting in the Red Zone, where the buffalo roam, the mother tongue is the language of cost cutting and revenue generation—the language of value.

Three Languages: Becoming Multilingual

Because the languages are a concept that most salespeople are aware of but don't know how to use as a tool, we offer this analogy.

There is a huge push nowadays to call higher in the organization. But calling high is not the trick—anybody can do that. The trick is—what do you say? What do you say to senior level executives that will let them see you as a value-add, and not just a salesperson who is trying to peddle something? Worse, if they think you have little value, they will pass you to a lower level and you will have to really fight and claw your way back up to the senior level. How can you be a value-add in these senior sales calls? You speak the right language.

Let's assign a language to each of the three levels.

♦ Level 1: the manager level, let's assign "Spanish."

- ◆ Level 2: the vice president level, we'll assign "Russian."
- ◆ Level 3: the senior manager level, we'll call "Greek."

We now have the three languages, Spanish, Russian, and Greek that represent the three levels of management.

How many times have you prospected at the vice president (Russian) level? You usually have one hour or less to impress and generate interest for what you are selling. You have your presentation material, your PowerPoint presentation, you've rehearsed your speech, and you're ready to go. The presentation begins and you're quite pleased with how well things are going.

About ten minutes into the presentation, the vice president asks a question: "Excuse me, but this presentation is in Spanish. I don't speak Spanish very well. Why don't you give this presentation to John and Mary who work for me, since they speak Spanish much more fluently than I do?"

This is not exactly what he says, but it's what he means. You are still feeling okay because the vice president has told you to call John and Mary and you can reference the vice president to get the meeting.

But the bottom line is—you are speaking the wrong language. If you don't have a Spanish to Russian dictionary, you're out of luck and maybe out of a sale.

You prepared the call in Spanish, gave it in Spanish, and delivered it in Spanish. You hang out with Spanish buyers all the time, and you speak Spanish very well. That's great, but it doesn't work at the executive level.

The trick is not calling high. Anyone can do that. The trick is knowing what to say when you do call high. What do you say to create value at the vice president level and above so they won't send you lower in the organization? Speak the right language. Speak Spanish to a Spaniard, Russian to a Russian, and Greek to a Greek!

10

Sell to *Their* Values, Not *Yours*

Who asks a King for a penny?

—Vernon Howard

"Dad, I have to go to cheerleading practice and you have to take me now!"

If you're Dad, do you see any value for *you* in that statement?

"I'll be there as soon as I can."

"But Dad, I have to be there early . . . . "

If you have kids, you know how it works. Eventually, Brianna gets her way, drags you to the car, and off you go. She is frustrated and nasty because she found you difficult to motivate. You're not in the best mood either, because you can think of 1,000 things you'd rather be doing. No value has been added on either side.

Well, after awhile she gets smart.

"Dad, it's time for cheerleading practice. Mrs. Johansen will be there early, and she wants to talk to you about her taking us to cheerleading all next week."

What???

Now you're on your feet and dragging your daughter out the door because you sure don't want to miss an opportunity to run into Mrs. Johansen.

Value has been created. More specifically, the transaction now meets what we call the Value Criteria.

The Value Criteria

This tool has three elements: value, action, and time (VAT).

1. The transaction must have *value* to both parties.
2. It must be *actionable*. There must be some action that has to take place on both sides.
3. The action must happen by a certain *time* or within a certain time frame. "Soon," "ASAP," "in the next few months," and "by yesterday" are not specific times. They do not count.

"Time" actually figures into the VAT equation in more ways than one, as we'll see. Let's look at the factors individually.

Value

Value, in the prospect's mind, has five elements.

Return on Investment (ROI). Customers are greedy. They want their money back. As a matter of fact, they want more than their money back. They want two or three times their money back. Prospects look at the financial transaction first to see if it makes sense for them to get involved.

Time. Prospects will always pay for time. Increase uptime, decrease downtime, reduce overtime, speed up time to market—time really is money, and if you can tell a persuasive story about how you'll save them time, prospects will listen.

Risk. In Chapter 10, we discussed the values that shape the special languages spoken by vice presidents and senior executives—the languages of revenue, costs, and market share. But there is one more value underlying those. At the more senior manager levels, it is all about risk. ***Everything is about risk***. Make their decision more sure or less risky, and you will turn a prospect into a customer. Typical risks include:

♦ Competitive risks
♦ Pricing risks
♦ Geographic risks
♦ Political risks
♦ Product risks
♦ Delivery risks
♦ People risks
♦ Manufacturing risks
♦ Engineering risks
♦ Integration risks
♦ Basic risks of the business
♦ Legal risks

Risk is the sole reason for existence of an entire industry. Why do you buy life insurance, health insurance, car insurance, and homeowner's insurance? To reduce your risk.

TIP: Engage executives in conversations that focus on reducing risk. Decisions at the lower level are very black and white. At the more senior level, decisions are fraught with risk, which is why they get paid the big bucks. Ask the senior executive about risk, and they don't shut up.

Motivation. Understanding a prospect's motivation helps you create value. Motivation can be summarized as a desire that pushes us either *toward* something or *away* from something. Are your prospects running away from a pain, fear, or uncertainty? Or are they running towards a vision, a strategy, a goal? If they aren't doing one or the other, what do they need you for? You can find out their motivation by asking "why" questions. Why is the prospect taking the time to speak to you? Usually you'll get answers like these:

- ◆ My old one is broken. (AWAY)
- ◆ I want a new style. (TOWARD)
- ◆ I like the new features. (TOWARD)
- ◆ The one I have just doesn't do what I need to do anymore. (AWAY)

TIP: : Until you learn otherwise, assume that a prospect is in AWAY mode. Fully 70 percent of all prospects are motivated by AWAY reasons—they're looking to solve a problem that's causing pain, not to grasp a new opportunity. Sad, perhaps, but true.

Brand. Brand creates value. Shoppers pay more for Rolex, Polo, Ferrigamo, and Mercedes. Business prospects pay more for Intel, IBM, Michelin, and Mont Blanc, since brands create pull. What can your brand do for the prospect? Better yet, what can your brand do for their brand so they can sell more widgets?

TIP: : Value is NOT about spewing your "value proposition" all over the table. Prospects don't care about your value proposition. What they care about is *their* value proposition. Help them with *their* values, and you have struck gold. The only way to do that is to ask them about their values. What is important to *them* about ROI, time, risk, and brand? Your canned spiel describes these things in *your* terms. Leave it in the can.

Action

"Yes, I can see your point and I agree it would make me more money. I am just not in a position to do anything right now."

For value to be realized, there must be some action you and the prospect can take to make it happen. Just to agree there is value, and then agree that nothing can be done to achieve it, does nobody any good.

No action, no value. Therefore, no action, no sale. Create a sense of urgency, usually using time or risk, and then request that the prospect do *something* to move the deal closer to fruition—even if it's only to agree to let you call back on a certain date in the future.

Time

We said that to meet the Value Criteria, the action in a transaction must take place within a specific time frame. We also said that time is one of the building blocks of value—customers will pay you to save them time. (That's why FedEx makes the big money.)

To take things a step further, time comes in three tenses: past, present and future. Your prospect's values in any situation will have to do with one of those tenses. The prospect's motivation is either:

◆ **Restorative.** The prospect merely wants to restore something to the way it was in the past: "I just want to get back to where we were before this computer virus hit."

◆ **Opportunistic.** The motivation is to take advantage of a present opportunity: "Well, since I'm buying these tires today, getting the oil changed will save me another trip . . . and it's on sale."

◆ **Forward Looking.** The prospect wants to invest in something now, so it will pay dividends in the future. "I really don't need these Happy New Year party hats in March, but at 75 percent off, I'll get them and use them next year."

Value, action and time are what prospects care about. That's what you should be selling to. How do you do it in a cold call? By asking questions as soon as possible:

◆ "What do you see as the biggest risk facing you and your company in the next few months?"

◆ "What are your current time problems in getting your product to market? Do you see a value in getting to market sooner today? What about six months from now?"

◆ "If you could save 20 percent of your inventory carrying cost, would that be of value to you?"

Those questions are a heck of a lot better than statements like:

◆ "We can save you time and money."

◆ "We have the best product on the market and we can boost your profits."

◆ "We have the hot solution that everyone wants now."

Click. Dial tooooooone.

11

Don't Sell *Stuff*, Sell *Solutions*

If there is a better way to do it, find it.

—Thomas Edison

"Solutions" has become a silly word in the high-tech age, in danger of losing any meaning whatsoever. Every company that sells anything related to computers calls itself a "solution provider." The word "solutions" appears so many times in these businesses' self-descriptions that it's often impossible to figure out what in the world the company actually makes or does.

Annoying as this may be, the computer industry has the right basic idea. The problem is just that it has mistaken an action imperative for a labeling issue. If you want to sell solutions to important customer needs instead of just selling *stuff*—and regardless of your industry, believe us, you do—it isn't merely a question of hanging a "solutions" label on your company or your products. It's a question of *how you sell*.

A friend of ours was in the trade show business. Her company organized and sold "mini-trade shows"—essentially tabletop displays on six-foot tables. Her company would rent a ballroom in a big hotel, set up thirty or forty six-foot tables, sell table space to vendors, send out about 5,000 invitations to targeted buyers, and act as the conduit between buyers and sellers.

Great concept. Just one problem: Try to sell a six-foot table to the vice president of marketing at a $500 million high-tech company. Why would he or she care about a six-foot table at a five-hour show at some hotel in Newton, Massachusetts?

When her sales team tried to sell tables to marketing vice presidents, their calls rarely got through. When they did connect, and they started selling the value of the table and the value of the buyers coming to the show, they made slow and painstaking headway.

Then her sales team got smart. They stopped selling six-foot tables. They started asking the vice presidents (VPs) about their marketing and customer strategies, and what they were trying to accomplish. After they covered those issues, the next questions they asked were: "What are you doing at the local level?" and specifically: "What are you doing to follow up your major trade show activity at the local level?"

The sales team thereby made their six-foot tables part of the VP's larger strategy. If VPs wanted to get all the benefit of the millions they were spending on major trade shows, it made sense that they also needed a low-end, local strategy. If a company plans to invest $2.2 million in trade shows next year in the hope of making more millions, wouldn't it be wise to earmark $50,000 for a local follow-up effort?

The overall solution VPs were looking for was an answer to the question: What is the smartest way we can invest a few million to earn more millions? By making themselves part of that solution, our friend's sales team found it a whole lot easier to sell six-foot tables.

Now, certainly the VP can unplug our friend's low-end solution at any time and replace her with another local trade show company. But that would involve time and risk. This small a piece of a $2.2 million investment isn't worth the time and certainly isn't worth the risk.

The upshot: Our friend's company sold more six-foot tables and held onto their customers longer when they stopped selling tables and started selling part of a larger solution. That's the trick. And that's the mind-set with which a Knock Your Socks Off prospector approaches every cold call.

> **TIP:** If you can't sell the whole solution to a customer's problem, sell a piece of it. But never sell a six-foot table.

Solution Box

Salespeople love to prospect for a need. They believe that if they can find a need and meet that need, they will make a sale. True enough, as far as it goes. But knock your socks off prospecting asks you to cast a bigger net to increase your chances of gaining the prospect's interest. With a bigger net you can catch more fish. The idea is to create some leverage.

Instead of asking if they have a need for your product or service, ask prospects what they are working on today. What are some of the current issues they're struggling with, and what are they doing about these problems?

If you want to be the entire solution to a customer's need, you must understand the need. But even if you can offer only a piece of the solution—which is far more common—you have to understand what the entire solution would look like. What is the whole of which you'd like to be a part?

By questioning the prospect, you build a solution box. The solution box allows both you and the prospect to envision what the entire solution would look like, and what role you could play in bringing it about. It also helps you communicate your honest desire to help the prospect solve an important problem. For a major or complex sale, you would rarely be able to build an entire solution box with a prospect during an initial cold call. Some or most of this work likely will take place during one or more follow-up calls. But the original cold call will be more effective if you know to begin with:

1. You're not selling a six-foot table.
2. Your objective during the cold call is to gain the prospect's permission to let you help build a solution box, probably during future calls.

There are three things to remember about building a solution box:

1. Be inquisitive. Remember, it's the customer's solution, not yours. Ask open-ended questions that encourage the prospect to talk and talk and talk.

2. Be quantifiable. The more facts and figures you get, the better. "Good," "soon," and "more" add no clarity for the salesperson or the customer. "Ninety-five percent," "two weeks," and "500 more" are quantifiable terms that have value.

3. Be top down. Discuss the whole solution, not just your piece of it. And look at things from the prospect's perspective. What is the overall problem? How will it be solved? Only when that is clear will your individual piece of the puzzle fall into place.

> **TIP:** Don't start selling while you are building a solution box with the prospect. If you're really trying to identify a solution that will create value for them, why would you start hawking your piece of the puzzle before you know what the whole puzzle looks like? This is a sure way to shoot yourself in the foot. The rule is, the less you say at this stage about what *you* can do, the better.

Finally, try to strike certain words and phrases from your vocabulary when building a solution box with the prospect. Here are some common phrases that undermine a salesperson's claim to be working with the prospect on a solution to *his* problem and not just trying to sell him something:

- ◆ We can help you.
- ◆ We have a unique . . . .
- ◆ We now can offer . . . .
- ◆ That is one thing my company . . . .
- ◆ I am sure you will see . . . .
- ◆ I know this is a perfect fit.
- ◆ I need to tell you . . . .
- ◆ I have an exceptional . . . .
- ◆ We are better.
- ◆ My company . . . .
- ◆ I . . . .
- ◆ My . . . .
- ◆ Me . . . .

Words that put the focus of the conversation on the salesperson rather than the customer need to be drop-kicked from our sales vocabulary. Better words and phrases are:

- ◆ What you . . . .
- ◆ You said . . . .
- ◆ Yes, you can, and have you . . . .
- ◆ Have you ever thought about . . . .
- ◆ Have you considered . . . .
- ◆ What would it be worth to you?
- ◆ How would you . . . .
- ◆ Where would you put . . . .
- ◆ When would you like to implement . . . .
- ◆ Why would you want to . . . .

The more questions you can ask, the more you keep the focus on the prospect. And the more you concentrate on the overall solution before getting down to your piece of it, the more value will be created in the prospect's mind. Is this because you have woven a diabolically clever mirage? No. The reason the prospect perceives more value is because if you do all this, the value is really there.

12

You Sell Change

Come to the edge, he said.
They said, we are afraid.
Come to the edge, he said.
They came.
He pushed them . . . and they flew.

—Guillaume Apollinaire

Companies need to change. People need to change. The list of maxims and sayings that make the point would fill a book longer than this one.

- ◆ "Without change, the world will pass you by."
- ◆ "If you are not changing faster than the environment, the end is definitely in sight."
- ◆ "What was good enough to get us where we are will not be good enough to get us where we need to go."

When it comes to prospecting, and to selling in general, two things are especially relevant about change.

- ◆ People and companies need to change.
- ◆ People and companies HATE to change.

TIP: The challenge isn't just to help the customer solve a problem. It's also to help them through a change.

65

Why is this so important? Because no matter what products or services your company has to offer, every time you contact a prospect the thing you are selling represents some kind of change.

Here is the most useful and productive attitude with which a Knock Your Socks Off prospector can approach the thorny issue of change:

The Change Seven

1. This company/buyer needs to change.
2. They hate change.
3. I can probably help them change and get what they really want.
4. They first have to recognize they need to change.
5. They then need a solution to make the change happen.
6. They need to see the value in changing.
7. How can I help them?

This is a world apart from a prospecting approach that begins with, "Hey, whatever I'm selling, they need it." The seven statements on that list are "pulling" the buyer toward a desired goal. The "Hey, they need it" approach is pushing the buyer. And nobody wants to deal with a pushy salesperson. The thing that every successful salesperson is really selling, always, is a change that adds value to the customer's current situation.

From Here to There

Every prospect we call upon has a current way of doing things—a current process. They're usually pretty happy with this process; otherwise, they'd have changed it before now. They have something that works. They're getting a reasonable return on their investment in it. That's why the graph shows that the "current process" line is going up (Figure 12-1).

The "value solution" line on the graph represents the thing you believe you can do to help these people. The difference between what they are doing now and what they can do if they change is the "value difference." Your job is to help them come up with metrics—guesses, if necessary—about what that value difference would be worth to them.

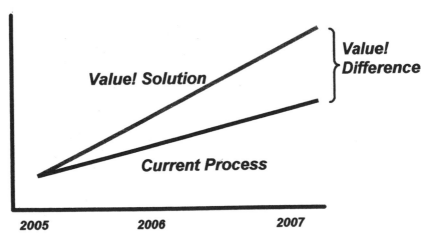

Figure 12-1. Value solution process.

This isn't an alien process for them. They're constantly looking for value differences already. They are reengineering, changing processes, retooling, and upgrading all the time. Your goal is help them see—and quantify—the value difference that your solution has to offer.

Use change as a lever to get into these companies and start the ball rolling. Someone has to start it, so why not you?

13

Execution:

The True Art of the Sale

Just do it.

—Nike Footwear slogan

Anyone can come up with all kinds of strategies to make a sale. It is the salesperson who makes the leap, the one who actually tries to execute the ideas, who wins the day. There are four Knock Your Socks Off secrets to execution.

1. Have a positive passion *about them.*

Very few things are as infectious as a positive passion. But it's not believing in your company or the strength of its products that's important. Your passion has to be for the value your product or service can provide for the prospect.

The difference sounds small, but it is huge. A lot of salespeople believe strongly that their companies and products are terrific. Only a few reserve their passion for what makes a deal terrific from the prospect's point of view, not their own. Those few are the winners. They knock people's socks off.

Consider a guy we'll call Joe. He sells ceiling fans. He has sold fans for the same company for twenty two years. He is very passionate about his fans. He loves the quality of the materials used. He loves the precision machining. He loves the selection of styles he has to sell. He loves his fans' ability to blow more air than rival fans and the excellent reputation his company and its fans have enjoyed for as long as they have been in business. He knows all the features and benefits of each of his fans, and he can answer any question put before him. Joe truly believes that he sells the best fans money can buy.

All of that is wonderful. But if Joe really wants to knock their socks off, he needs to get past his own reasons to love these fans and direct his passion to the reasons why prospects might love them. Why does a prospect want a fan in the first place? (It's probably not because of precision machining.) What particular need will the fan serve? What is important *to them* about the qualities of one fan versus another? How will having a fan in a room allow them to enjoy their home more?

Joe believes he sells great fans? Swell. Now he needs to get passionately curious about how prospects might feel if they had a great fan. For positive passion to be contagious, it has to be *all about them*.

2. Be prepared.

Naturally salespeople need a thorough understanding of the features and benefits their company and their products have to offer. But the real trick is to be prepared from the prospect's perspective. What's on their mind? What worries them, takes most of their attention, makes their ears perk up when the subject is brought to the table?

Whenever possible, great salespeople do their homework about the issues the person they are going to be calling on faces on a daily basis. That way, the salesperson walks into the call prepared to discuss options in a conversation where both parties bring something to the table. The alternative is a conversation in which one party tries to talk about his needs (having been encouraged to), while the other tries to pitch a product.

TIP: How can you prepare yourself to discuss a prospect's needs on a cold call? If you are calling on a public company, the last two or three quarterly reports, available on its Web site, usually are good indicators of where time and effort are being spent. If it is a private company, insiders like administrators, marketing people, and current sales-people are good contacts. Outside the company, customers and competitors are always talking as well. The question is, are you listening?

3. Ask.

A key element in execution is to take the offensive. Ask. Ask questions, ask for help, ask for understanding. If you are really passionate about them and their needs, and if you've done your homework, prospects want to talk to you.

But don't just ask questions for the sake of asking. "So, Ms. Smith, what keeps you awake at night" is just as stupid as, "So, Mr. Jones, what are your current pain points?" You have to earn a seat at the asking table. That's where homework comes in.

♦ "Mr. Smith, based on your last quarterly report, it seems you are looking to increase your inventory turns, is that right?"

♦ "Ms. Jones, I talked to some of your people, and it seems that your company could really use a solution that would measure the success of new product launches. Is that right?"

♦ "Ms. Apple, you said that cutting time to market is your number one goal. What are you doing now to achieve that?"

4. Start from the next step.

Time and time again, salespeople begin a cold call only to have the prospect say something like, "Well that sounds good, why don't you call me back in a few weeks when I have time to talk?" A lot of salespeople feel good about this. They pull out their calendars and mark a date in a few weeks when they will call the prospect again. Hey, the guy invited them to, right? Obviously he'll take the call.

Wrong. What you just heard was a stall. Stalls can go on forever.

To prevent stalls and avoid dropping the execution ball, try to get prospects involved in a "next step" of some sort.

There are three great ways to do this. Give them homework, get a date, and call around.

- ◆ **Give them homework.** Give prospects something to do. Ask them to fill out a form, send an e-mail, or gather some information. *Warning:* We are NOT talking about the gambit where you send them a mountain of marketing literature and ask them to read it: "Mr. Smith, I'll send you all the information I have. If you can just review it . . . . " Who has time to review anything? Give them a simple assignment. Ask them to call someone, do something, answer a three-question e-mail to help you get better prepared. Get them involved in the start of the process.
- ◆ **Get a date.** Get a specific date of action. A good next step is not, "real soon" or "as soon as possible." Set a real date, one that shows up on your calendar. Then you'll be moving this sale along.
- ◆ **Ask if you can call around.** Before the cold call ends, tell the prospect that as a next step you want to do a little more homework. Ask who they would recommend you speak to in order to get some more information before your next conversation.

This gains involvement in a roundabout way, but you will have a concrete reason to call back in two weeks (you talked to some of the people the prospect recommended) and the prospect will have a reason to take your call (you were diligent in doing the homework that they gave *you*).

There is no one "right" way to execute a cold call. But prospectors who follow the advice discussed in this chapter may find, to their surprise, that cold calling is not as hard as they've always thought.

Part Two

The How-To's of Cold Calling

We have covered the fundamentals. It's time to move on. The chapters in this next section will look at some tools that can help you become a true Knock Your Socks Off prospecting machine.

To develop a style and procedure that will improve your cold-calling success in a consistent and lasting way, you have to break down the process into bite-size pieces and practice them. Following the "prospecting is an art, not a science" philosophy, the more colors available in your palette, the more types of painting surfaces you have to work with, and the more styles of art with which you're comfortable, the more flexible and successful you will be. To put it another way, you're better off with a lot of tools in the box than with only a few.

Remember, you're an artist. You don't have to do any of this "exactly by the book." However, we recommend that you take the following tools and start by trying them as we describe. Try to modify your style to work with the tool as it is presented. Then, after you have some practice time under you belt, feel free to modify the tool to suit your individual style.

It's like taking voice lessons. On the first day of class, everyone will try to imitate their favorite singer—Frank Sinatra, Cher, Nora Jones, Pavarotti. Some of them are even pretty good at it. But the instructor puts a stop to this nonsense right away. The voice coach tells the students to sing the notes and scales as they are written, with no ad libs and nobody else's "style." The coach knows that after students have sung the scales and exercises a number of times, their own natural style will emerge. Once the student has incorporated his or her own style with the basics, that's when real music is created.

Everyone has their own style, and in selling, being comfortable is important. But even if you have to move a little outside your comfort range at first with any of these tools, please give it a try. Then move back into your comfort zone, taking the technique with you.

We'll present the tools by walking through a cold call. What do you do at the start of a cold call? What do you do in the middle? And what do you do at the end?

14

Your Thirty-Second Speech

All my successes have been built on my failures.

—Benjamin Disraeli

The Beginning

Do you find that the hardest part of a cold call is getting started? The next five chapters contain ideas and techniques that make it much easier to gain a prospect's interest quickly—and to set the stage for a productive conversation. We'll even tell you how to leave messages that have a far greater chance of being returned.

It all starts when you prepare and refine a thirty-second speech to open your cold calls . . . .

Riinnnng

"Hello?"

"I am looking for Mr. Jacobs, please."

"This is he. May I help you?"

'Yes, my name is Ramon Lewis. I'm with the EZ Building Company. If you have a minute, I'd like to tell you about a special we are having this month that could be of help to you."

"Yeah? Tell me more."

Oh, oh, here it comes. The old "show up and throw up." Triggered by "tell me more," Ramon is going to talk for the next 24 hours. At least, it will seem that long to the prospect. Ramon is doomed. Why? Too much talking.

> **TIP:** : You have four to six seconds to make a good first impression. And you have thirty seconds, tops, before the prospect wants in on the conversation. For crying out loud, let them in.

Time to jump in the water. Up to this point we have been doing the necessary spade work to lay the foundation for an effective cold call. Now we're going to make one.

The first tool we need is a good thirty-second speech—an introduction we can use every day to begin a cold call. Once we get the format right, we can fine tune it and personalize it.

Every cold call should start out with a thirty-second speech. And a thirty-second speech follows the Rule of Three.

The Rule of Three

For most people, the limit of short-term memory is seven digits (or units), plus or minus two. If we feed bullets of information to prospects, we start overloading them at five. By nine, we've lost practically everyone.

But why risk overtaxing anybody at all? Throttle back and feed information to prospects in units of three—well inside the borders of short-term memory. It's no accident that we love things in three's:

◆ A-B-C
◆ 1-2-3
◆ Good—Better — Best

Craft your thirty-second introductory speech with three points:

1. "Who are you?"
2. "What's in it for people like me?"
3. "What's in it for me?" (WIIFM.)

The "me" in points two and three is, of course, the prospect. WIFFM is *always* about the prospect.

Here's a quick summary of these three points.

Who Are You?

Introduce yourself. Make it short and sweet—a kiss on the cheek, not a lingering embrace. State your name and company. Then move on. If you spend more than three seconds here, you are kissing way too long.

What's in It for People Like Me?

Explain why the prospect should bother to talk to you. Tell them a few things about what you may be able to do for them. Give them a point of reference about who you are and what you do. You aren't an invader from Mars, you're in the widget business.

Warning: Do not tell them, and tell them, and tell them about all the things you do, hoping that eventually you'll hit upon something that actually interests them.

NOTE: THE QUESTION IS **NOT,** "WOULD YOU BE INTERESTED IN FEATURE X OF OUR NEW ACCOUNTING SOFTWARE PROGRAM?" THAT TELLS THE PROSPECT THIS CALL IS ABOUT YOU, NOT ABOUT THEM.

What's in It for Me?

Buyers want to be lead. You just gave the prospect a general idea of how you might be of help. Now zero in on a specific interest. How? By asking. Your thirty seconds are up, and it's time to let the prospect talk.

Ask a question that gets prospects thinking along the lines of action and that lets them tell *you* what might be in it for them. What is important to them right now? Based on your homework, experience, or knowledge of the industry, you can probably make a pretty good guess about what a specific WI-IFM might be. For instance, if you're talking to a vice president of finance, you might ask a question about accounts receivable issues or the timeliness of financial reporting.

That's the outline of your thirty-second speech. Now let's construct one (Figure 14-1).

Your First Thirty-Second Speech

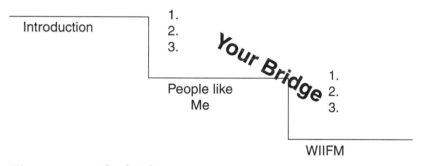

Figure 14-1. The bridge.

Your introduction lasts three seconds:

> *"Hello, Mr. Smith, I'm Ramon Lewis with the ABC Company."*

That's it. Anything more would put the focus on you, not the prospect. Move immediately to an explanation of what you do and why the prospect might care. Following the Rule of 3, the "What's in it for people like me?" section of the thirty-second speech has no more than three points:

> *"Hello, Mr. Smith. I'm Ramon Lewis with the ABC Company. We are the leading supplier of widgets in*

the world, we have been in business for over 20 years, and Our job is to improve our customer's competitive position."

That's enough to give the prospect a frame of reference. Now get them interested and involved. To do that, first "cross the bridge," and then ask a good question.

NOTE: DURING ROLE PLAYS IN SALES TRAINING SEMINARS, SALESPEOPLE WHO START FOR THE FIRST TIME WITH A THIRTY-SECOND SPEECH OFTEN SAY THAT THEY FEEL AWKWARD. THE SPEECH FEELS TOO "CANNED" TO THEM. BUT THE SALESPEOPLE PLAYING THE ROLE OF BUYERS LOVE THE SPEECHES. IN FACT, THEY SAY THEY BECOME ANNOYED WHEN A CALL DOES *NOT* START WITH A THIRTY-SECOND SPEECH. INTERESTING?

Your bridge phrases include:

◆ "You are probably wondering . . . .
◆ "We hear from executives in your position who want to know . . . .
◆ "Many people ask us . . . .

Run-of-the-mill salespeople blow it at this point by finishing the bridge phrase with something that is about themselves or their companies, not about the prospect.

Bad bridges phrases:

◆ "Mr. Smith, you are probably wondering what my company can do for you."
◆ "Mr. Smith, executives like yourself want to know how I can help them."
◆ "Mr. Smith, people ask me all the time, 'Bob, how can your company help me?'"

Well, no, as a matter of fact Mr. Smith wasn't wondering about you or your company at all. The awful truth is that except for your mom, practically nobody is wondering about you right now. Most people on the planet can go fifteen minutes at a time without wondering about your company.

Mr. Smith was more likely to be wondering about the following (we call these "good bridge phrases").

- ◆ "Mr. Smith, you are probably wondering, How can I speed up my time to market?"
- ◆ "What is the best way to maximize my current revenues from a distribution partner?"
- ◆ "Mr. Smith, when we talk to sales executives we hear questions like, How can I help my sales team improve at calling on higher levels in customer organizations?"

Notice that those good bridge phrases include preliminary WIIFM questions designed to start the prospect thinking: "Yeah, I do worry about that, and I'd also like to get a handle on . . . ."

This is the prospect's first step toward real involvement in the conversation. Now we must encourage them to take actual *ownership* of the conversation. How? We summarize and flip.

 ## Summarize and Flip

Summarize the bridge questions you just put out there (no more than three to a customer, please), and then flip the conversation to the prospect. It's their turn to talk.

> *"These are questions we hear all the time, Mr. Smith,* (summarize). *But before we talk about those,* (flip) *what are the key issues that* **you** *are looking at over the next few months?"*

Following is an example of a good thirty-second speech. This example uses three general WIIFM statements and three bridge questions that aim at specifics. Your own speech might include fewer of either, but never *more* than three. And general statements should never outnumber bridge questions— i.e., never three general statements and only one bridge question. Why? Because the emphasis always belongs on WIIFMs that are specific to the customer.

A Good Thirty-Second Speech

"Hi, I'm Tim Sparks with Falcon Filming. We do local videotaping of kids' sports events.

1. We help kids be better athletes by letting them watch and learn from their own efforts.
2. We help parents remember great memories.
3. We do this at a very reasonable fee, because we are filming many kids at the same time.

Many parents ask us:

1. How can I get my son or daughter on tape for a reasonable fee?
2. What kinds of things can kids learn from seeing themselves on professional videotape?
3. How much can my child improve at his sport by watching his performance on tape?

Those are great questions. But before we cover them, what besides home videos have you done to help your child become more competitive?"

Now that's a salesperson we'd listen to. (In fact, Skip Miller did. He got some great videos and the improvement has been dramatic.)

15

Thirty-Second Variations:

The Opening

You have to concentrate on one idea at a time.

—Robert Collier

The format we just looked at for a thirty-second speech is an excellent one. But you will want to tweak the specific wording depending on the circumstances of an individual cold call. Tweaking begins with the opening—the way you introduce your thirty-second speech. Here are some variations to consider.

The Reference

Did you get the prospect's name from a mutual acquaintance? Great, there's your opening:

> *"Hi, Mr. Smith. My name is John Marks. Bob Grandee from ABC Interiors made me promise to give you a call."*

Caution: The "reference" opening counts on your prospect to know Bob Grandee or ABC Interiors and to think favorably of them.

The "May I Ask?"

"Hi, Mr. Smith, my name is John Marks from the XYZ Shoe Company. May I have thirty seconds of your time to ask you a few questions?"

The "May I ask?" opening works well when:

♦ You are calling on prospects who know of you or use a product/service like yours (Nike to Athletes, Mont Blanc to businesspeople, Gerber to moms).
♦ You have name recognition among your buyers and a respected brand (Ferrari, Virgin Atlantic, Hewlett-Packard, Starbucks).
♦ You have a product, service, or technology that is the hot thing (I-Pod by Apple, *Harry Potter* books by Scholastic).

The Headline

The headline is a good opening when you believe the prospect already has an interest in the thing you want to talk about.

"Hi, Ms. Smith, my name is John Marks. As you may know, interest rates are starting to go up."

"Hello, Mr. Banner, my name is John Marks. The holiday season is weeks away . . . . "

The Agreement

Seek the prospect's agreement about a premise relevant to your call before you start the thirty-second speech:

"Ms. Forth, can we agree that if you wanted to buy a new home, one of the first things you need to do is to find out how much your current home is worth today?"

Ask Permission

Here's a question about cold calling that has been debated for years. Should you ask the prospect's permission before starting your speech? Or should you just go for it?

> *"Mr. Thomas, my name is Steve Stone, and I represent the DFG Company. Do you have a few seconds for me to tell you about . . . ?"*

Sometimes the answer will be "no," followed by a dial tone. So what do you think? Should Steve ask for those seconds or just try to take them and hope the prospect doesn't hang up on him anyway?

Our feeling about the matter is best expressed by the story of Debbie and Carl. Debbie was a veteran salesperson for a company we'll call Ace Systems. She was assigned to mentor Carl, who had a few years of selling experience but was new to Ace.

Debbie spent the better part of two days telling Karl about the company, its target market, its products, its competitive advantages—the works. Like many veteran salespeople with established clients, Debbie was a little rusty on prospecting, but she thought a few prospecting calls before the end of the day would set the stage for tomorrow, Carl's first full day of selling.

Carl got on the phone and made his first cold call with Debbie right there.

> *"Mr. Guinta? Hi, this is Carl Holt from Ace Systems. Is now a good time to talk? OK, when would be? Great, I'll call you back then, thanks."*
>
> *"Carl, what did you do?" Debbie asked in horror. "You NEVER ask permission to hook the prospect. You just go for it."*
>
> *"I always ask permission," Carl replied. "It's the polite thing to do."*
>
> *"Well, you'd better pick up some new habits," Debbie told him, "because asking permission to talk to someone is old school. You will never get that guy back, I guarantee it. Let's call it a day, and I'll see you tomorrow."*

The next morning Debbie arrived at her office and found Carl at her desk, getting ready for a day of prospecting.

> *"What are you doing in my office?" she demanded.*
>
> *"I like it better than my cube," he explained. "Thanks again for all your help."*
>
> *"Carl, who said you can use my office and my desk?"*
>
> *"You did."*
>
> *"I did????"*
>
> *"Sure. Yesterday you said that asking permission is old school."*
>
> *"I wasn't talking about my office, I was talking about prospecting."*
>
> *"Your office, their office, in person, over the phone—what's the difference? If I don't have to ask permission to come into a customer's office, why do I have to ask permission to come into yours?"*

Debbie got the point. So should you.

16

Thirty-Second Variations:

WIIFM?

Success is the sum of detail.

—Harvey Firestone

No prospect will agree to talk with you for longer than thirty seconds because of the fascinating things you have to say. It isn't the statements you make that will pique their interest. It's the questions you raise. They have to be questions for which prospects actually want an answer—for their own reasons, not yours.

The summary and flip at the end of your thirty-second speech has to make prospects think. And what they must think is, "Hm, maybe there *is* something in this for me" If they don't think that, the call is over.

As you remember (don't you?) the summary and flip is where we flip the conversational ball to the prospect with an open-ended question about his needs or concerns. The "bridge" questions—or "what's in it for me" (WIIFM) questions—with which we lead up to the flip are crucial because they prime the thought pump. If one or more of our WIIFM questions don't hit the prospect exactly where he lives, at least they should start him thinking about a related question that *does* keep him awake nights.

So let's look a little more closely at WIIFM questions.

WIIFM Questions

Why do we make such a point about framing these as questions, not as statements? Because statements neither encourage thought nor invite conversation. Questions do both.

"Mr. Smith, you are probably wondering:

♦ How can I speed up my time to market?
♦ What's the best way to maximize revenues from my distribution partner?
♦ How can I help my sales team get better at calling at higher levels of customer organizations?"

"Yeah, I do wrestle with those questions," Mr. Smith thinks, "but I think about them in a slightly different way. And that first question is more important than the others because . . . ."

See? The prospect has begun to think about his own concerns. That's all any prospect wants to talk about with a salesperson for longer than thirty seconds. Now, when you flip him the ball, he'll be ready to catch it.

Variations on the standard WIIFM questions in your thirty-second speech can arise from three general areas.

1. Your Homework. If the homework you have done before calling on this prospect suggests some specific or unusual WIIFM questions, use those instead of your generic queries.

2. Things You've Done in the Past for This Prospect's Company or for Companies Like This. If your past experience with this company or with a particular industry gives you any ideas about how to zero in on WIIFM questions that hit specific hot buttons, tailor your questions accordingly: "Mr. Smith, when I worked with Ms. Jones of your company, she had questions like . . . ." Mentioning your prior connection also gives you added credibility. You aren't a total stranger, you're someone who has worked with Ms. Jones.

3. Issues Geared to the Prospect's Role in an Organization. For instance:

- ◆ Sales managers are always concerned about forecast accuracy.
- ◆ Senior executives are always concerned about risk and time.
- ◆ Accounting people are interested in the accuracy of the numbers and how long it takes to get them.
- ◆ All businesspeople are interested in value, action, and time (see Chapter 10 on VAT).

TIP: The closer your WIIFM questions can come to nailing the Big Question that is actually on a prospect's mind, the more willing he will be to start guiding the conversation when you hand him the steering wheel in the summary and flip.

17

Summary and Flip

Everything in life is a progression of steps.

—Scott Reed

The whole point of a thirty-second speech is to engage prospects enough that they start talking. When the first thirty seconds of a cold call expire, it needs to become a conversation, not a monologue. If the summary and flip at the end of your speech fail to start the prospect talking, it makes no difference how terrific the rest of the speech was. The call has crashed and burned.

Here are some pointers about pulling off a good summary and flip.

1. Use *we, us,* and *you,* never use *I.*

In your summary statement, avoid the word *"I."*

Wrong: "These are great questions, Mr. Smith, but before I get into those, I want to . . . ."

Who cares what you want to do? The prospect hasn't asked you out on a date.

Right: "These are great questions, Mr. Smith, but before we get into those, could you . . . ."

Much better. This encourages two-way communication. You've been doing all the talking to this point, but now you're asking him to participate.

2. End with a question.

We already explained that the "flip" at the end of your thirty-second speech is an open-ended question. But it bears repeating: *The thirty-second speech ends with a question—*

91

always. It's the prospects' turn to start talking. You need to let them know that. The question gives them their cue.

3. Make the question relevant.

Want to show prospects that you're wasting their time? That you're on a fishing expedition for a "need" you can pretend to satisfy? That you're just delivering a canned spiel? That you don't really know or care about their situation or their problems? Then go ahead and ask questions like these:

Wrong:

"So, Mr. Smith, what keeps you awake at night?"

"So, what are your pain points?"

"So, what is your area of need?"

You have to do a lot better than that. And you can. Make the question relevant to the person you're talking to.

Right:

To a senior executive: "What are the areas of most risk to you as you enter the new fiscal year?"

To a vice president of marketing: "Where do you see your growth opportunities coming from in the next three to six months?"

To a design engineer: "What are the projects you'll be working on soon that will be the most interesting for you and your company?"

Tailor your flip question as closely as you can to the things you know about the prospect's role and concerns. After all, the premise of your call is that you can help them in some way. Before they'll take ownership of the conversation, prospects need to feel that you know enough about what they do—or what they care about—to be worth talking to.

A cold call is a work of art. Use your art to get the prospect involved enough to start talking.

> **TIP:** The more questions you ask about prospects' specific concerns, the more they will talk about their needs. The more they talk about their needs, the likelier you will uncover one you can serve.

CAUTION: YOUR NATURAL TENDENCY WILL BE TO INTERRUPT AND ANSWER THE NEED, SINCE THAT'S WHAT YOU GET PAID TO DO. FIGHT IT. THE PROSPECT WOULDN'T HAVE BROUGHT UP THIS NEED UNLESS THEY HAD A POSSIBLE ANSWER IN MIND. IF THEY ASK YOU QUESTIONS, RESPOND WITH SOME QUESTIONS ABOUT THEIR QUESTIONS. THIS IS THE "ASKING" TIME OF THE SALES CALL. THE ANSWERING TIME COMES LATER—MUCH LATER.

18

Leaving a Message

Chance favors the prepared mind.

—Louis Pasteur

A good thirty-second speech often will work practically intact when you contact prospects by e-mail or fax. And if the prospect doesn't answer the phone, the speech becomes your voicemail message.

The only really *necessary* modification is to the summary and flip that follows the "what's in it for me" (WIIFM) questions. Instead of saying, "Before we talk about these . . . ." you might say something like, "Do questions like these concern you? Please contact me at _____."

At the same time, however, we need to recognize what we're up against when we leave messages instead of speaking to prospects directly. Sales messages that pile up in e-mail boxes are called spam. Those that arrive via fax are called junk faxes. Voicemail messages from salespeople are "telemarketing calls." Prospects regard them as a plague. They're looking for reasons to delete your message, not for reasons to return it. And they have hair triggers.

Somehow your message has to cut through the clutter. It has to make prospects pause and think before their fingers can hit the "delete" key. In an e-mail, this applies not only to the actual message but to the subject line as well. When you check your e-mail and discover twenty or thirty messages, the first thing you do is delete the ones that look like spam, right? The people *you're* trying to reach do the same thing.

95

Here are two quick techniques to help you leave messages that will get read or listened to—and that might therefore generate a response.

The *YOU* Headline

The benefit to prospecting by e-mail or voicemail instead of by regular mail is speed. Most people check their snail mail once a day, but they check their e-mail and voicemail ten to twenty times a day.

But that speed is also our enemy because it prompts the hair-trigger "delete" instinct. We need prospects to slow down and hear what we have to say. To stop them in their tracks, use the word *you.*

- ◆ "Your phone was . . . ."
- ◆ "You have said . . . ."
- ◆ "Just read that you . . . ."

"Did I say that?" the prospect thinks. Or, "Oh, yeah, I did say that, didn't I." Either way, we have made them stop and think. That's a good thing. Even better, we have asked them to think about *themselves,* not about us. *You* is a much more powerful tool than *I.*

> **TIP:** Record the thirty-second speech you use for cold calls via voicemail. You should hear the words *you* or *your* two or three times more often than *I* or *me.* You'll be surprised how many times you unconsciously use the word *I.* But the prospect hears it every time, like fingernails on a chalkboard.

The Reference

As we said earlier, any time you can turn a cold call into a warm call by referring to someone the prospect knows, do it. This becomes doubly powerful in an e-mail or voicemail message.

The prospect's old friend Fuzzy told you to call? Say so immediately—in the subject line of your e-mail or the opening of your voicemail message. The prospect's finger will pause over the "delete" key. A picture of Fuzzy forms in the prospect's mind. A sense of responsibility to Fuzzy is created.

> *"If I don't call this guy back, I'm sort of betraying good old Fuzzy. Besides, Fuzzy wouldn't tell anyone to call me unless he was OK."*

People the prospect knows make the best references. But people you know, even if the prospect doesn't, can be useful as well.

People you know—your current customers, industry leaders, the President of the United States—can lend you extra credibility. The more impressive their names, the better: "Mr. Smith, at a White House briefing last week, the president singled out your company as an example of . . . ." Though you don't say it, what comes across to the prospect is, "Hi, Mr. Smith, the president and I are calling to find out . . . ."

People they know make the best references because if you and the prospect both know the same person, then you sort of know each other.

What you say is: "Holly, I was talking to John Fuzzer the other day, and he told me to contact you."

What the prospect hears is: "Hi, Holly! Good old Fuzzy called and said we should all get together at the bar tonight and shoot the breeze, us being buddies and all."

All right, maybe the prospect doesn't hear quite that much. But by making the association with Fuzzy you have put yourself into the same club as the prospect and her friend.

If you're sending an e-mail, put Fuzzy's name in the subject line. "Fuzzy asked me to contact you" or "Blame Fuzzy for this message." Guilt by association can be an ally.

Slow the Trigger Finger

The goal of both these techniques is to get prospects to slow down or stop before they automatically hit the "delete" key.

They have to do that before they can read or hear—and maybe respond to—your message. Use these tools to get them out of the fast lane of the speedway and onto a side street—if not into your driveway. You're competing with a lot of noise out there. Sales are only made when the prospect takes the time to listen.

19

The Buying Process

If not you, then who?
If not now, then when?

—Hillel

The Middle

If you're one of those salespeople who finds that the hardest part of a cold call is the beginning, congratulations. You're past it. The thirty-second speech carried you through. The prospect had enough interest to answer your flip question instead of hanging up or telling you to call back after Bastille Day.

Now what?

In the middle part of a cold call, the task is not only to maintain and strengthen the prospect's interest but to start building a relationship.

It's time to begin the actual sales process that will allow the buyer to make a decision to purchase from you or not. This chapter outlines that process. The following chapters will go into more detail about how to handle the middle section of a cold call.

Buying decisions are made according to a process. If you can walk hand in hand with prospects through that process, they are far more likely to decide in your favor. In this chapter, we'll look at the overall process. Then we'll quickly introduce two concepts—control and action—that we'll dig into in more detail later.

The buyer and the seller both have roles in the buying decision process, which looks like this.

Buyer's Steps

Let's look at the buyer's side of the process. Following are the steps any buyer goes through in deciding whether to make a purchase (Figure 19-1):

   1st Step: They have an *initial interest*. That's what your opening thirty-second speech created, and good for you. At this point, however, there are still 500 other things that interest your prospects more. To get seriously interested, they need additional information.

   2nd Step: The prospect now wants to be *educated*. Feature/benefit selling techniques are usually used here.

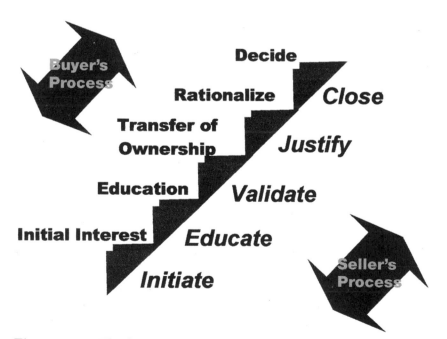

Figure 19-1. The buying decision process.

3rd Step: If the education phase goes well, prospects begin to *transfer ownership*. They can picture the product as a solution to a real need. They begin to *sell themselves* on its virtues.

4th Step: Now having a good idea what the product is, potential buyers enter a *rationalization* phase. They come up with objections that must be addressed:

- ◆ Have I looked at all the competitors I need to?
- ◆ Do I really want to make this purchase decision now?
- ◆ Can I afford it at this time?
- ◆ Do I really look twenty years younger with this new hairpiece, or do I look like a doofus with a bad rug?

5th Step: The prospect *decides* whether to buy. Yes or no? That's it.

TIP: You probably will not take the prospect through the entire Buying Decision process in an initial cold call. Be aware, however, that there *is* a process the buyer goes through. You are at the Initial Interest step. Your goal is to get to the next step. One step at a time, okay?

Two factors will be especially important during the middle of a cold call.

Control the Call

Remember how happy we were when the prospect began to take control of the conversation and steer it toward their own needs by answering the flip question at the end of the thirty-second speech? We're still happy about that. But there is a paradox here, because in the middle of a cold call, *you* need to gain and maintain control.

In the beginning the goal is to create interest and get prospects to talk about themselves. This gives you an opportunity to learn more about them before you start selling. But that doesn't mean you can drop the reins for the rest of the call and just go along for the ride. You're the one who must always know what the next step is—the goal that you and the buyer are aiming at during each phase of the process. That means you have to be the guide.

What's the goal you're aiming at in the middle of a cold call? To move up the buying-decision ladder from Initial Interest to Educate.

Create Action

During the middle of a cold call you want to create action. This might mean that the prospect agrees to your proposal of a next step—a face-to-face meeting or a follow-up meeting, for instance. Or it might mean you agree that there is no fit and no next step is needed at this time. Either way, you have created action. If you aren't going to move further up the sales path with this prospect, thank him for his time and make your next cold call. See? Action.

Next we'll look at these two factors in more detail in Chapter 20.

20

Who's Driving?

Effective communication is understanding what the other person understood.

—Tony Robbins

In the middle part of a cold call, after the thirty-second speech, who is in control of the process? In Chapter 19, we learned that ultimately it must be the salesperson who guides and steers the conversation. This is a buying process, and the salesperson is the one who knows what the next step must be at every point if the process is to continue.

But control is a paradoxical issue. For one thing, buyers always have the control that finally matters, because they're the ones who will say yes or no to the sale. For another thing, the buyer always must feel in control, regardless of who is leading or following at any given point on the path toward a buying decision.

In the middle of a cold call, the challenge is to remain in control of the vehicle while allowing prospects to feel that they're doing the driving. There are two basic ways to keep control while seeming to give it up:

1. Hand the steering wheel to the prospect.
2. Change the perspective.

Hand Them the Wheel

Throughout this book we have stressed the importance of words that put the focus on the prospect, not on the salesperson: you, not I; we, not me.

Handing control to the prospect is partly a matter of language.

> Bad: "Ms. Hyde, I think we should talk about that some more, and then I can figure out if I can help you."

> Better: "Ms. Hyde, why don't we talk about that some more, and when we're done, we can determine our next step."

> Best: "Ms. Hyde, why don't we talk about that some more, and when we're done, you will be in a position to determine your next step."

The bad statement is, of course, all about the salesperson. It is not important in a cold call what you think or even how much you want to help.

The better statement is mutually consenting and far more powerful.

The best statement is more powerful still. It not only hands control to the prospect, it takes her into the future. "You will be in a position . . . " leads Ms. Hyde to the future, and lets her go by herself, if she wants to, without the salesperson for

company. But "to determine your next step" puts a stopper on that future. We're not talking about the rest of Ms. Hyde's life, only about the next rung on a buying ladder. She is in charge, and all she has to do is make a decision about a next step—not a decision about whether to buy anything.

The best statement puts Ms. Hyde behind the wheel in a nonthreatening, low-pressure driving situation. Heck, she's cruising through Vermont on a bright fall day, watching the leaves change color.

Give them control. Take them to the future. Define the next step so they know how far they have to go. Then let them hit the gas pedal and go.

Diving Lesson

Remember the first time you had to jump off a diving board? We'll bet someone was there to coach and encourage you— your parents, some older kids, or a swimming instructor. They showed you how high the board was and how far you were going to fall until you hit the water. Maybe mom walked you out to the end of the board while dad was treading water in the pool below, ready to grab you. Then, when you were ready, they let you take that first jump.

Who was in control every step of the way? But after you made the jump, who yelled, "I did it!"?

Change the Perspective

The second way to maintain control while giving it up also has to do with the language we use. But the words we choose are shaped by the perspective we bring to a situation.

Yes, this is that I, we, you stuff again. You can follow some of the recipes in this book by monitoring your language closely at all times. But the language piece will fall into place much more easily and naturally if you aren't forced to maintain constant vigilance over your pronouns. Change your perspective, and the pronouns will follow.

There are three perspectives we all look through: the first, second, and third.

In the first perspective, we see a situation through our own eyes. The world unfolds from an *I* viewpoint.

Even when we say things like "I see what you mean" or "I hear what you're saying," we are speaking from the first perspective. Who is the subject of those sentences? I am. I may be concerned with your point of view, but what I'm thinking about is me and my reaction to your view.

In the second perspective, we are actually engaged or absorbed in seeing things through the other person's eyes. We're more likely to say: "You said you were thinking about . . . ."

In the third perspective, we see things more or less objectively from both our point of view and the other person's points of view. It's as if we're arbitrators at a baseball players' salary meeting, seeing both the players' and management's sides of the argument.

Salespeople have a tendency to come to cold calls in the first perspective. The more they believe in the value of their products, the worse the problem can get: "If I can just take everything that is in my head, and put it into your head, you will see the obvious benefits of what I'm talking about."

Ah, yes. Trouble is, you need to get prospects thinking and talking, instead of just listening to you yack about your features and benefits for as long as they're willing to stand it. You would also like prospects to understand what you're saying. In fact, you would like them to become engaged and absorbed by what you're saying.

If you want them to regard you from the second or third perspective, you have to do them the same courtesy first. Who's going to steer the conversation away from the first perspective if not you?

"I think a good place to start . . . ." (first perspective)

"What I would like to help you with is . . . ." (second perspective)

"People like yourself sometimes ask . . . ." (third perspective)

"You might ask . . . ." (second perspective)

"If we look at the big picture . . . ." (third perspective)

"Why don't we . . . ." (third perspective)

By switching to the second or third perspective, we get prospects involved and convey the feeling that they are in control. One more time: Prospecting is always about the prospect. Bad things happen when a cold call is about the salesperson instead of the prospect.

> **TIP:** : Knock Your Socks Off prospectors cultivate the ability to see things from all perspectives. They can hold a conversation that moves among different perspectives to involve a prospect. They don't just speak *at* the prospect.
>
> Try having a conversation with your kid tonight in which you take their side totally. See what jumping perspectives is like and what it does for rapport!

Invite prospects into a two-way conversation by displaying the second and third perspectives. And when they're up on the diving board, guide them, don't shove them. Tell them the water is fine, and let them jump. You will have a great cold call.

21
Transfer of Ownership

Always think in terms of what the other person wants.

—James Van Fleet

Have you ever applied for a job and done so well in the interview that the hiring manager started to sell himself on your qualities instead of making you sell yourself to him? Maybe it began when you expressed a reservation:

You: *"I'm not sure I'm right for this job, Mr. Smith. You say you're looking for an aggressive salesperson. I like to go after new business, and I like getting a good margin for my sales. But I believe in working **with** customers to find solutions that will really benefit them. That's especially true when I call at higher levels of an organization."*

Mr. Smith: *"But Susan, that's exactly what I want! When I said 'aggressive,' I didn't mean . . . . "*

That's what "transfer of ownership" looks like in a job interview. If Mr. Smith starts telling *you* why you're the right person for the position instead of vice versa, a powerful shift has occurred. When the same thing happens in a sales call, you are knocking their socks off.

There is no cool brochure or terrific PowerPoint presentation that can compare with the beauty of it. When prospects begin to sell themselves, they are imagining all the things they can do with what you are selling. And their imaginations are more relevant, if not more active, than yours.

Common Problem

When prospects are selling themselves on the product, the salesperson usually is trying to sell too. The prospect is asking questions and listening for answers. That's good. But this causes stress and pressure for most salespeople. They feel like Mount St. Helens ready to explode. They have to get a word in—a sales pitch, something, *anything* about their company or one more feature of their product. They just *have* to do a little spewing . . . er, selling.

What's the right thing to do instead? For Pete's sake, let them sell themselves! Switch roles. You are no longer playing the tuba, trying to be the loudest instrument in the orchestra. You have become the conductor. So conduct. Answer the questions. Direct the cold call toward the next step in the sales process.

The $64,000 question is, how do you get to a point in a cold call where prospects will start selling themselves? Here are two tools that will help.

Ask Questions

You have heard it a thousand times. Here it is for the 1,001st. The best salespeople learn how to ask questions that get prospects involved. They do this instead of "selling" in a manner that has the salesperson doing all the talking and the buyer doing all the listening.

You already know how the "selling" approach works: Heck, if prospects only understood your product or service as well as you do, they would rave about it, just like you do. But because they don't know enough to appreciate its glory, you're going to tell them as much as they'll sit still for. And don't leave a single feature off the table, because, hey, you never know what might grab them.

That's the wrong way. The right way is to ask questions. When you do, use a structured approach. We recommend one called Ask/Tell/Ask:

◆ **Ask prospects what they need right now.** What is important to them at this moment? What is it they really would like to have to make their jobs or lives easier, or better, or more complete? (Remember, you're now in the middle of the call. They know you sell apples. They aren't going to tell you they want pumpkins, motorcycles, or trips to the moon.)

◆ **Tell them you have heard them by paraphrasing what they said.** Just let them know what you have understood; don't tell them what you and your company can do for them.

◆ **Ask: If they had a solution in hand, what would it look like?** What would they do with it? How would they be using it right now?

TIP: To transfer ownership and get prospects to sell themselves on a product, ask questions. Great questions begin with Who, What, Where, Why, When, or How. These magical questions are open-ended. They can't be answered with a yes or no. They cause the prospect to think. This is good. If they are thinking; they usually will think of questions to ask you.

Two-Way Solution Box

We described a solution box in Chapter 11. The best way—in fact, the only way—to construct a solution box is to make it a two-way project.

Imagine that you and the prospect are building something together: a bridge, a ball field, a car, a house. You are combining your resources to obtain a desired end. Naturally, both parties will wind up with responsibility for certain tasks that must be accomplished to reach the final objective. But who's objective is it? The prospect's. That's the focus. When building a solution box, there is no need to focus on *your* solution—not if you want to transfer ownership to the buyer.

Sam coached a Pop Warner football team that needed a field on which to practice and play. The high school field the team had been using would no longer be available.

Sam was in charge of finding a new facility. He approached another high school that was convenient to most of his players. He offered quite a bit of money to let his son's team use the field.

"Considering how badly we already need a new field, we really don't want anyone else chewing it up, so thanks but no thanks," said the principal, declining the offer.

Far from being discouraged, Sam saw an opportunity and jumped on it. He got donors lined up and worked with the school and community to refurbish the football field. The job was done in six months. The local newspaper ran a story on the new field. The story talked about what a wonderful job the school's boosters had done and how happy everyone was about the project.

Not a word was mentioned about Pop Warner football or the fact that Sam had been responsible for raising almost 95 percent of the money. That's because Pop Warner football was not in the school's solution box. The school's solution box was full of needs to get a new field built by August, in time for its football team, soccer teams, and band to begin the fall season. And by golly, they made it! But oddly enough, the field opened on the date when the Pop Warner team needed it..

Now, the donors and the people at the school knew perfectly well that Sam's personal interest had to do with his own team. But Sam focused on the school's needs. The school, of course, focused on its own needs as well. That created a two-way solution box. Pop Warner football was strictly an after-

> thought, as far as the school was concerned. But
> Sam got exactly what he wanted out of the deal.
> And without his "selfish" interest in Pop Warner foot-
> ball, the high school would not have a new field.

Focus on the prospect's goals and objectives. Find a solution to the prospect's problems. Make sure everyone knows what's in it for both sides, but keep the emphasis on the prospect. That's how you transfer ownership.

22

It's About Time

Time has no meaning in itself unless we choose to give it significance.

—Leo Buscaglia

Time is a wonderful and terrible thing. Everybody wants to spend more of it doing things they enjoy and less of it doing things they dislike. Busy people always want more of it, period, just so they can get everything done. Deadlines are always too close. Delays are always frustrating. People (including prospects) also have different personal orientations toward time.

Time can be used in many ways to help you sell. There are three tools that are particularly useful in the middle of a cold call to keep prospects talking to you about things that *they* want to talk about:

♦ Time dimension
♦ Time direction
♦ Time demo

Time Dimension

Everyone has a time dimension—a basic orientation toward time. Some of us live "in time." The rest live "through time."

"Time-in" people live in the present. They have relatively little concern for yesterday or tomorrow. These are the people who get to work on a Monday, look at their calendar, and ask,

"How did my schedule for today get so busy?" When they are house hunting, they look for a home in move-in condition.

A "time-through" person sees events and ideas in the context of yesterday, today, and tomorrow. When asked to schedule an appointment, a time-through person couldn't imagine looking at a day in their PDA without knowing what was going on at least the day before and the day after—if not the month before and after. When house hunting, time-through people are less concerned with what the place looks like right now than with what the house will look like when it's occupied or when they throw their first party.

Eighty percent of humans are time-through people. But we have a tendency to sell as if everyone was a time-in person:

♦ "What this does for you . . . ."
♦ "If you want this right now . . . ."
♦ "Currently, we are offering . . . ."
♦ "Today, if you can . . . ."

To communicate effectively with a time-through person, we should use phrases such as:

♦ "Last time you tried something like this . . . ."
♦ "Over the next few weeks, you will see . . . ."
♦ "And by this time next month . . . ."

How do you tell which time dimension a prospect has? Listen to how they talk with you. A time-in person is interested in the here and now, period. A time-through person is interested in history (yours and theirs) *and* in the present situation *and* whether you are going to be around tomorrow.

How Do You Know Which Time Dimension You Have?

Close your eyes. Think of your last birthday. Where do you see your last birthday? Point somewhere in space. Where do you see your next birthday? Go ahead, point to it in space. Where is your last wedding anniversary? Point to it. Where do you see your next anniversary? Point.

Do that before reading further.

To time-in people, what's behind them is *behind* them, and what's ahead is *ahead*. They will point behind themselves to past events and directly forward to future events.

Time-through people will tend to point from left to right, or right to left, rather than forward and behind themselves. Because time is a continuum and needs to be controlled, past, present, and future are all essentially in front of a time-through person. But yesterday is to my right, today is in front of me, and tomorrow is to my left (or vice versa). Everything moves through time, of course, but nothing is behind me, out of control, or out of mind.

Time Direction

A second time element that can help you in the middle of a cold call is time direction. Time has three directions—past, present, and future. Every prospect's key needs relate to one of them. We mentioned this in Chapter 10, but here's a slightly different look.

- ◆ **Past: Restorative.** Something has gone wrong, and they want to put things back to the way they were. "We spent $2.2 million on that sales-automation system, and it takes longer to book an order. I would pay money just to get our response time back to where it was."
- ◆ **Present: Opportunistic.** They have a current need. Something is knocking on their door right now, and it is pressing. "If I don't get a solution in place in the next few days, it will be my head!"
- ◆ **Future: Preventative.** They will spend money now to avoid pain in the future. Putting money in an IRA or a college fund is a preventative decision. "I'd better start saving now or my kid might not be able to go to college."

Figure out where the prospect is by asking time-sensitive questions, such as:

♦ Is this an immediate need? Why?
♦ What has happened, or what goal are you trying to achieve?
♦ What's going on that makes this a top priority?

Odds are, the needs revealed by the answers will break down in terms of time direction like this:

Past – 20 percent
Present – 60 percent
Future – 20 percent

These percentages hold true except with vice presidents (Russians) and top-level executives (Greeks) (see Chapter 9). They live in the future, or they get called in to fix something. So their percentages are:

Past – 30 percent
Present – 20 percent
Future – 50 percent

Play the percentages when you are cold calling, whether by letter, e-mail, voicemail, or face-to-face.

Time Demo

A time demo is a tool to help prospects envision a solution to a problem or need (hopefully your solution) and to induce transfer of ownership. It works like this:

First, discuss today's reality. Describe the problem or the situation as the prospect has explained it to you. This lets you check your understanding of the prospect's position and ensures you both see the current reality in the same terms.

Then, discuss what tomorrow's reality should be. What would their life be like if they already had your product and it solved the problem for them? Ask how they would feel?

We call these Polaroid or snapshot answers. You will hear answers such as:

"I'd feel great."
"It would be super."

Many salespeople know how to get this far, but then they stop, happy with their progress. Heck, they just got the prospect to agree that it would feel great to own the product they're trying to peddle. What could be better than that? Well, there's hopes, dreams, and desires, there's what's next,. and there's future benefits.

Ask the prospect, "Once this problem was solved, what would you do next?" In other words, discuss the possibilities that would open up for the prospect if tomorrow's reality were already here and your product had solved their current problem.

"Well, if my current need were solved, I would be able to get involved in that other project I have been trying to find the time for."

"I'd be spending weekends at home rather than working most Saturdays and Sundays."

"Now that you mention it, if I used your widget to get the elephant out of the room, I could . . . . "

When prospects start talking about their hopes, dreams, and desires, your have arrived in a wonderful place (Figure 22-1). At this point, you shut up. They'll figure out on their own that if they want to realize their hopes and dreams, they'll have to go to tomorrow's reality. To get there, they'll have to buy a widget from somebody. Since you're the one who led them through the time demo, it probably will be you.

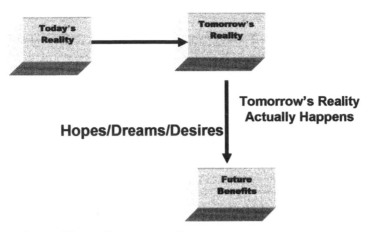

Figure 22-1. Time demo sample.

Typical Future Benefits Comments

Once a prospect's attention shifts from today's reality through tomorrow's reality on to future benefits, here are some things you might hear:

> *"If I had this TV in my living room right now? Well, I wouldn't have to fight my kids over what I want to watch. I'd be able to go to the other room and watch what I want for a change."*

> *"If this project were implemented, the return on investment would fuel our product development team and give them about a three-month head start. My president would be really happy about that."*

Those future benefits are now part of your proposal. Maybe the prospect could achieve them by buying from a different supplier, but because you were the one who had this discussion with them, they will anchor the benefits to your solution. Remember: Prospects are going to have this future benefits conversation with *somebody*. Why not you?

To keep prospects engaged in the middle of a cold call, play with time. Make time your ally, and you'll knock their socks off.

23

Summarize, Bridge, Pull

The relationship begins after the sale is made.

—Theodore Levitt

The End

The conclusion of a cold call does not mean the finish of the sales process. On the contrary. The end of a cold call is the *start* of the real sales process.

We have reached a critical juncture. The prospect is on the cusp between a first conversation with a stranger and a relationship that might last for years. If you followed our advice so far (ahem!), this has been an unusually interesting and productive conversation from the prospect's perspective. They are ready to take a next step of some kind.

But what will that step be? Who will determine it? If you don't, the prospect will—and that creates problems galore. Our discussion of how to end a cold call starts with the issue of control.

The key to ending a cold call successfully is to make dead certain that you remain in control of the buying process.

TIP: : The end game of a cold call is all about taking control of the next step.

Kim felt great. She had prepared for hours, and on her third attempt she got through to the right person—a high-level (Russian) contact. Over the past ten minutes, the cold call had

121

uncovered some real needs that Kim and her company could help with.

The prospect had said at the start of the call that he only had a few minutes. Kim could sense that something else was pressing. She wanted to end the call and get an appointment.

Kim: *"Mr. Gluck, we have covered quite a bit, and it sounds like we may be able to help you with your inventory situation."*

Mr. Gluck: *"Yes, what you have sounds interesting. Why don't you call Fred Spork, my inventory process manager, and see if you two can figure something out."*

Kim: *"That sounds great. Thanks again for your time."*

Well, hey, what's wrong with that? Kim got a reference. She gets to call Fred, and she has the power to say, "Your boss told me we should talk." She did well in the first place to get through to Mr. Gluck, and now Fred will call her back in the blink of an eye. She is well launched into the buy/sell process, isn't she?

One small problem: The prospect had all the control. It was Mr. Gluck who told Kim what the next step would be. And she's thinking, "If I do what the prospect says I should do, and I do it well, I'll get the order."

Yeah . . . maybe. But if she does, she'll be lucky.

Maybe Kim agrees with the old saying, "I'd rather be lucky than good." We don't. We'd rather be good. Because if you're good, you can repeat a success again and again.

 ## Summarize, Bridge, and Pull

Every cold call begins with a thirty-second speech. And every call should end with a technique called summarize, bridge, and pull (SBP). Here is how Kim could have used SBP to keep control of the next step in the sales process:

Kim:	*"Mr. Gluck, we accomplished a lot today. You said you wanted to lower your costs up to 20 percent by managing your inventory flow more effectively, you see this being implemented by the end of the year, and we discussed how we might be able to help. Would you agree?"*
Mr. Gluck:	*"Yes, I would. It has been a good meeting."*
Kim:	*"Great. So as a next step, let's sit down together. We'll learn more about what you really want to accomplish, and you'll learn more about what we do. At that point, you will be in a perfect position to determine if we should go any further. Does that sound good to you?"*

That's an example of a well-executed SBP. Let's take it apart to see the structure. Then we can build it back up.

A well-executed SBP has three parts:

1. They/you
2. Bridge
3. Next step

They/You

Summarize the discussion you just had, making sure to put the prospect's position first. Let us stress that: *Never put your own position ahead of the prospect's.* Start with an introduction statement, then go right for a they/you position statement.

Intro Statement and They/You Summary: `"Mr. Gluck, we accomplished a lot today. You said you wanted to lower your costs up to 20 percent by managing your inventory flow more effectively. You see this being implemented by the end of the year. And we discussed how we might be able to help."`

Bridge

Prepare the prospect to cross the bridge with you by asking a simple question: Do they agree with your upbeat summary of the call? Are you seeing eye to eye so far?

Bridge: "*Would you agree?*"

"*Yes, I would. It has been a good meeting.*"

Usually the prospect agrees because you merely summarized a conversation that just took place. All they're agreeing to is that, yes, they said X, you said Y, and it sounds okay so far.

If the prospect does not agree with the bridge question, you will uncover an objection that has to be dealt with. We'll discuss that in Chapter 24.

Pull—Next Step

Now, *you* propose the next step in the process, instead of leaving a vacuum for the prospect to fill.

Pull: "*Great. So as a next step, let's sit down together. We'll learn more about what you really want to accomplish, and you'll learn more about what we do. At that point, you will be in a perfect position to determine if we should go any further. Does that sound good to you?*"

Again, in most cases, the prospect will agree. For one thing, this would, indeed, be a logical next step. For another, it's a next step that promises to leave the prospect in full control: "You'll be in a position to determine if we should go further."

That promise is true. But in fact, you have taken control at the end of the call by determining what the next step will be. You have completed an SBP.

An SBP should be done at every meeting and after every conversation with the prospect. It's easy to lose control of a deal. It can happen in a split second. And it usually happens at the end of a meeting, when a prospect takes over and sends the deal in a different direction than you want it to go. You think it's just a detour. But this is no detour; it is a battle for the steering wheel.

Did the prospect grab the wheel before you got to the SBP? Did they derail the SBP somehow? It doesn't matter. You need to take back control of the next step:

"Mr. Gluck, we have covered quite a bit, and it sounds like we may be able to help you with your inventory situation . . . "

"Yes, what you have sounds interesting. Why don't you call Fred Spork, my inventory process manager, and see if you two can figure something out."

"That sounds great, and I'll do that. Then let's get back together and go over the results so you'll be in a position to determine if we should go any further." ("Because there is no way I'm getting off this phone without control of the next step in the process," is what you need to be *thinking*.)

Salespeople often end a cold call thinking they are in control, when in actuality someone else is pulling the strings. It isn't that you don't want to talk to Fred Spork. Of course you want to meet with him—he's the inventory manager. But don't be fobbed off on Spork as a dead end. Stay in charge of that future step. Summarize, bridge, and pull is a way to make sure you're in control of the meeting when the meeting ends.

Cautionary Tips

Here are some *don'ts*. These are things NOT to do at the end of a cold call.

◆ **Don't forget to follow the 3:1 Rule.** In your summary statement, always mention three of the prospect's concerns for every one of yours.

"Mr. Gluck, we accomplished a lot today. You said you wanted to (1) lower your costs up to 20 percent by (2) managing your inventory flow more effectively. You see this (3) being implemented by the end of the year. And we discussed (1 for you) how we might be able to help."

Stop right there and go to "Do you a*gree?*" Do not spend the next few minutes summarizing what you can do. You already did that during the call.

◆ **Don't ask the prospect what to do next.** This is sales at its reactionary worst. You're the one who made the call or asked for the initial meeting. You must know what the next step should be—or at least what you'd like it to be. (If you don't, figure it out before you ever make another cold call.) *You* suggest the next step—always.

◆ **Don't just follow the next step the prospect does suggest.** The law of sales control says that the buyer is always neutral. If you aren't controlling the sales process, someone else is. And that someone else usually isn't leaning in your direction.

◆ **Don't follow the buyer's process.** Some companies—and even some individuals—have a formal, complex buying process of their own. Some salespeople believe that if they jump through the hoops of this process better than anyone else, they will win the deal. This is nonsense. If it wasn't your process to begin with, it won't be yours at the end. The person who owns this deal will be the one who put the process together. Look for ways to route the train back onto *your* tracks.

"Sure Mr. Gluck, we can do that, and we will. A first step we may want to take before we get there may be . . . "

"That's a great idea. Before we do that, we should first . . . "

"That is a good process, and we'll follow it. As a first step to get there, why don't we have a meeting with you and your staff to discuss . . . "

Don't let that train start running away from you. Your train, your tracks; keep it that way.

- ◆ **Don't forget the bridge**. This is an easy trap to fall into. The bridge looks like such a small, inconsequential contraption, sitting there between summarize and pull. But leaving it out can ruin a sale.

"Mr. Gluck, we accomplished a lot today. You said you wanted to get your products through the development cycle 20 percent faster, and we discussed how we might be able to help, (no Bridge) so I think a good next step would be . . . "

A bridge is always needed, and you must walk hand in hand with the prospect across it. You can't cross it first and then yell to the prospect to come along. If you do, prospects will feel they are "getting sold." So don't forget to pack your bridge phrases:

- ◆ Would you agree?
- ◆ Does this sound about right?
- ◆ Is this what you thought we covered today?
- ◆ Are we of the same opinion on this?
- ◆ Do you concur?

Summarize, bridge, and pull is a powerful tool in the prospector's bag. Every cold call—indeed, every sales call—requires a next step. Without an SBP, control of the sales process is up for grabs.

24

Handling "NO!":

Which "No" Is That?

No can be the beginning of a beautiful relationship.

—Mark Twain

When a prospect or a suspect says "no" to an appointment, to a callback, or to the next step you suggest at the end of a cold call, as discussed in Chapter 23—it's important to know which *no* you are dealing with.

There are four kinds of *No's*, an idea we first heard articulated many years ago by sales training guru Larry Wilson.

The Four *No's*

1. No Trust. The prospect may have a need, but something about you, your approach, or your proposal has led them to feel that you can't meet the need. The prospect doesn't trust you and/or your company to do what you say you will. Salespeople from small companies selling to prospects in large companies encounter this doubt all the time. It's a legitimate fear—and one you particularly need to anticipate when cold calling to a prospect who is unlikely to have heard of your organization before.

2. No Need. You may not be speaking to a legitimate need. If that's the case, you aren't talking to a real prospect, so move on. But it also may be that you have not sold the prospect on the idea that they have a need—even though you're convinced the need is there. When that happens, it's called denial. Doctors run into denial all the time. "Geez, Doc, it's just a headache. Brain surgery? I don't think so." Sometimes your first sale is selling the prospect on their own need.

3. No Help. Sometimes there is a legitimate, important need to be met and the prospect knows it. But something about your proposal or your company or your call feels "off." They don't see your proposition or product working the wonders you're promising. You have a solution, they have a need, but they don't see the two meshing. And they aren't ready to let you convince them otherwise.

4. No Hurry. There is a need, you have a good idea, and it probably will work. But what's the rush? Somehow, you and the prospect don't see eye to eye on the urgency of doing something. Rearranging one's retirement plan to downplay stocks, particularly technology stocks, didn't seem an immediate need to most investors in early 2000. It is often incumbent on the Knock Your Socks Off prospector to create the motivation to act in one's own best interests.

Knowing Your *No's* When You See Them

1. The "No Trust" *No.*

Trust is the bedrock of business transactions. If the prospect doesn't believe you, or suspects your intentions, you can never build a relationship—or sell him a stick of gum. If the prospect has never done business with you or heard of your organization—especially in today's low-trust business environment—it is a reasonable guess that no trust might be the issue. If your company has been in the headlines for a negative reason, you can be sure trust will be an issue.

Signs and Symptoms of No Trust

♦ "I would have to know more about you folks . . . ."
♦ "That's a pretty big claim."
♦ "I've never heard of you."
♦ "I'm pretty happy with who we are doing business with today." (Even though I don't have a clue why.)
♦ "I don't really know."

Just about anything that puts the prospect in the "I don't know you and you have not earned the right yet to take up more of my time" mode—yep, that's the trust thing.

2. The "No Need" *No.*

Sometimes a prospect just doesn't need what you're selling—even if your homework says they should. They may, for instance, have just purchased a product or service similar to yours from a competitor. (Hard as that may be to believe!) Sometimes, however, the words "we just bought one" are simply a way to get you off the phone. You need to check out the reality of the statement.

Five Signs of Denial or a "No Need" Stall

When you hear one of these five statements from a prospect, it's even money they haven't actually evaluated their need lately. Or, if they have, they don't want you to make life complicated by forcing them to take action on the need.

- ◆ "We're happy with what we have."
- ◆ "We're not in the market just now."
- ◆ "We aren't ready for an upgrade."
- ◆ "We haven't gotten all the value out of the Acme 4000."
- ◆ "It is not a priority for me right now." (Even though the holes in the dam are getting bigger, and the flood is coming.)

Any of these forms of *No's* should prompt you to probe on.

3. The "No Help" *No.*

No Help is the *No* that says you and the prospect are connecting about there being a need, but not about the solution. Or at least, not about the likelihood that you and your organization are able to provide a viable solution.

Symptoms of a "No Help" *No*

You and the prospect are probably in the no help tango when you hear phrases like these:

- ◆ "We would never need anything this complicated."
- ◆ "I don't see how your product meets a need for us."
- ◆ "We already do business with someone who can do that."

Getting a prospect to talk here requires you to focus on a solution the buyer can see. Ask, "What could our product do better?" or "How do you see your needs changing over the next year in this area?" You need to move the prospect off their current center. If you are not the lead dog on a dog sled, the view never changes, but the starting point has been left behind a long time ago.

4. The "No Hurry" *No.*

TIP: If a prospect says "we just bought one" and you think you're getting shined on, say something like, "Great, may I ask which widget stretcher you settled on?" Followed by, "May I ask what attracted you to the Acme 4000?" At the very least, you'll be learning something valuable about a competitive product/service.

The classic "no hurry" *No* comes from the life insurance prospect who figures he'll live forever or the health insurance prospect who avoids thinking about illness—at all costs. They both understand the product and the need for it. They may even trust the organization and the salesperson to deliver it effectively. Where do things break down? At the "what if" barrier: "What if I never get ill? What a waste of money this would be." And "Everyone in my family lives a long time. If I spend dollars on this, I'm really dumping money down a hole."

Sounds of the "No Hurry" *No*

The no hurry *No* is probably at the root of an appointment, or callback, or next step refusal when you hear things like:

- ◆ "We'll need to do that eventually—but . . . ."
- ◆ "I'm sure that when we really need to do that, you'll be on our list."
- ◆ "If you'd like to send me something, we'll keep it on file."
- ◆ "We're just not ready to . . . ."
- ◆ "I'll get back to you when . . . ."

To counter this one, recognize that the real issue is change. Change is inevitable, but no one likes to change. Here is where you ask about changes the prospect is facing and gain agreement that they need to change faster than they think. They are stuck in neutral on the tracks of change and don't see that train coming.

Plan to hear the four kinds of *No's* throughout the prospecting process, and be ready for them—especially at the end of a cold call. If the summarize-bridge-pull technique explained in Chapter 24 produces a *No*, it most likely will be one of these four.

Part Three
Following Up

You did it! You got your ducks lined up using the Fundamentals in Part One, and you executed a successful cold call in Part Two. You are well and fairly started on the road to a sale. Now what?

Are we finally going to let you hammer the prospect into submission with the old feature/benefit hard sell so you can close this deal and make some money? Sorry, but no.

People don't like to be "sold to" or "sold at." Your job isn't to try to control the prospect, it's to maintain control of the sales process. That's the kind of control that was important at the end of your cold call. It remains important now.

In Part Three, we'll take you through the next few steps and offer some tools that will help you reap the fruit of the hard work you put into this sale so far.

135

Knock Your Socks Off prospecting is not just about who can get the appointments. It's about who can maintain tho momentum. Following up after a successful cold call is like going on a first date after you have talked on the phone—or to a job interview with the hiring manager after you've made it through the pre-screening process. Both parties will be checking each other out carefully.

It comes back to controlling the steps of the sales process. Do that, and you'll probably win the sale. Here's how.

25

Call #2:

Second Thirty-Second Speech

Coming together is a beginning. Keeping together is progress. Working together is success.

—Henry Ford

"Dennis, Bob, Gail, and Ted, it's good seeing you folks again. Thanks for having me back. Last time we talked, you said you wanted to:

1. Change the travel agency you are dealing with by the end of the year.
2. Make sure the new agency has a worldwide presence.
3. Insure you get 24/7 service without paying additional charges.

"Today, you wanted to discuss:

1. How our agency can meet your specific needs, especially the international problems your travelers have been running into overseas.
2. What our online support function looks like.
3. How our pricing structure works.

"Is this correct? Any changes? Have any other items come up since we talked? Good, then let's get started *with today's meeting. First, I want to make sure we are on the same page. If all goes well today, a good next step we should be thinking about is to sit down and put together a rough schedule of how the transition would take place. We should have that done by the end of the month. Is this okay with everyone? Great, so let's get to today's agenda."*

After you have talked to a potential customer for the first time, you are no longer cold calling. But you're still prospecting—at least in the sense that you aren't yet dealing with an established customer.

The second call on a prospect is often as tricky as the first cold call, because this one is all about control of the sale. The prospect wants control and so do you.

The above conversation is an example of a well-executed thirty-second speech for sales call #2 and beyond. It recognizes the prospects as the ones in charge of the deal. It lets them know that their concerns have been heard—but keeps the salesperson in control of the next step.

Broken into its component parts, that second thirty-second speech looks like the schematic in Figure 25-1.

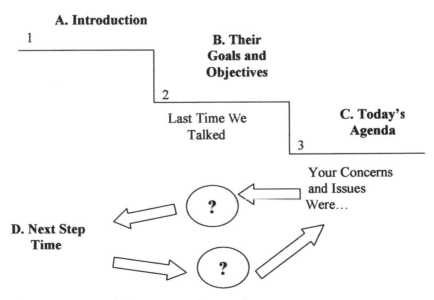

Figure 25-1. A thirty-second speech.

Taken step by step, this speech is very easy to master and modify for your own needs. Let's look at its parts one by one.

Introduction

Plain and simple. Acknowledge everyone and thank them for their time: "Dennis, Bob, Gail, and Ted, it's good seeing you folks again. Thanks for having me back."

Their Goals

Here is where you make them feel they are being heard. Statements like, "What I would like to do," or, "What my company can offer . . . " are wrong at this time. If prospects are still talking to you after the initial cold call, the reason is because they have a goal they are trying to satisfy. By reminding them of it, you let them know you're here for *their* reasons, not just for yours. When you state their goal, over and over, prospects will say to themselves, "This person is listening to me. They understand what I'm trying to do."

This is much better than the prospect saying, "Yep, that's what this character said he could do for me—or *to* me, more likely."

> *"Last time we talked, you said you wanted to: (1) Change the travel agency you are dealing with by the end of the year; (2) make sure the new agency has a worldwide presence; (3) Insure you get 24/7 service without paying additional charges."*

See? No sales pitch hiding in there, and nothing yet about what you can do for them or to them. You're simply restating the goals they stated to you, demonstrating that you were listening and that you want to be sure you understand them correctly.

Today's Agenda

Now get specific. Based on their goals and the understanding you arrived at in the initial cold call, here are the topics you expect they want to cover today. Since you are jumping in the water now, make sure there is still water in the pool by asking if they have any new concerns they'd like to talk about.

> *"Today, you wanted to discuss: (1) How our agency can meet your specific needs, especially the international problems your travelers run into overseas; (2)what our online support function looks like; (3) how our pricing structure works.*

"Is this correct? Are there any changes? Have any other items come up since we talked?"

Next Step

Don't wait until the end of the meeting to clarify what the next step in the process will be. Do it right up front, before you get down to business. And make sure to attach a specific time to the next step. This gives everyone a map that tells them where they're going. And, of course, it leaves you in control of the process. Since you obviously have listened to them and understand their goals, they'll usually be happy to let you take the lead by suggesting the next step.

> *"Good, then let's get started with today's meeting. First, I want to make sure we are on the same page. If all goes well today, a good next step would be to sit down and put together a rough schedule of how the transition would take place. We should have that done by the end of the month. Is this okay with everyone?"*

> **TIP:** Way too often, the senior decision maker in the meeting has to leave early. They'll say something like, "I have to go. Bob and Mary will finish this up with you." And whoosh, they're out the door. Then you have to struggle to get them back into the process. Use your opening thirty-second speech to establish a next step while the senior exec is still in the room. That beats chasing them down the hallway later.

Use this blueprint to construct a thirty-second speech for every call after the first one. See what happens? You successfully kick off the meeting. You make the prospects feel they have been heard. You get your agenda for the meeting approved. You uncover hidden questions and new agenda items. You reach agreement on a next step. And the meeting starts with you in control of the beginning and the end. Not bad at all.

26

TripTik®

Success is a journey, not a destination.

—Anonymous

"Are we there yet?"

How many times have you heard that phrase coming from the backseat? It drives you nuts, but look at it from the kids' point of view. They don't know where Los Angeles is, six hours is an eternity to them, and "we're still in Arizona" is the same meaningless gibberish it was twenty minutes ago.

Kids on a car trip need a way to orient themselves in time and space and to give them a sense of control in an unfamiliar situation. When we were kids, the American Automobile Association (AAA) came up with a tool for that job. It was called a TripTik®.

A TripTik® is a series of map pages strung together in book. If you want to drive from Albuquerque to Los Angeles, the TripTik®'s first page takes you from Albuquerque to a point maybe 100 miles west. Then you turn the page to a map of the next 100 miles, and so on. A neat idea, and a great way to orient curious kids.

 ## The Sales TripTik®

Buyers in the early stages of an unfamiliar sales process are in a similar position to those kids in the backseat. A sales Trip-Tik® is a great prospector's tool that can serve the same function for them. It gives the prospect and the salesperson a tangible map to follow by outlining the steps or milestones in the sales process (Figure 26-1).

Buyers want to be led, and they want to follow a process. Show them in the early going what the process will look like.

TripTik®

Prospect Company: _____

Contact Name: _____

Initial Sales Call Date: _____/_____/_____

Installation Date: _____/_____/_____

What are the steps we have taken together so far?

1. _____

2. _____

3. _____

What are the next buy/sell steps do you want to take to make sure a decision is made?

		Complete?	
		Yes	No
1. _____		☐	☐
2. _____		☐	☐
3. _____		☐	☐
4. _____		☐	☐
5. _____		☐	☐

Insert steps the prospect is going to be taking on their own.

Update this Trip-Tik after every sales call.

Figure 26-1. A sample sales TripTik®.

Figure 26-1 is an example of a simple sales TripTik®. "Next steps" might include things like:

♦ Finish up requirements.
♦ Live demonstration completed.
♦ Final proposal presentation.
♦ Final vendor selection.
♦ Purchasing and legal review.

Work out the action items with the prospect so that you're going down a buying path together—and the prospect isn't going down a buying path with somebody else.

Figure 26-2 is a more impressive example of a TripTik®. It's a visual representation of the whole buying process. It's clear. It can be put up in a cube or office. It can have the prospect's logo on it. You can work together to change the dates or action items. You can create multiple versions, such as a technical TripTik® and an executive TripTik®. A picture is worth a thousand words, and this is one picture that can really make a difference.

Create custom TripTiks® in conjunction with your prospects—don't just go away and do it for them. If they're actively involved in building and adjusting one of these, they will logically follow only one buying process. If you get some major push back, you know you have a problem. Why? Because you are helping them do their job and minimizing their risk. Who wouldn't want to use a tool like this? A prospect who is not really qualified, that's who.

TIP: Seventy percent of all prospects are visual learners, which means they find visual aids very helpful. Create TripTiks in a multicolor picture format, not just as a list of words. A picture is worth 1,000 words, and control of the sale.

The TripTik® thus is a qualifying tool as well. Use it to weed out those *maybes* that are never going to happen. Use it to own the process, own the deal, and work as a partner with real potential buyers.

ABC Company TripTik®

Start Date

Decision Date (I-Date)

| June | July | Aug | Sept | Oct | Nov |

Actions to Be Taken by Month

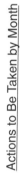

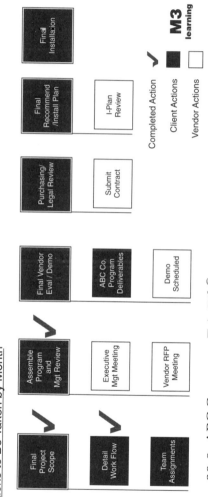

Final Project Scope

Detail Work Flow

Team Assignments

Assemble Program and Mgt Review

Executive Mgt Meeting

Vendor RFP Meeting

Final Vendor Eval / Demo

ABC Co. Program Deliverables

Demo Scheduled

Purchasing/ Legal Review

Submit Contract

Final Recommend /Install Plan

I-Plan Review

Final Installation

✔ Completed Action

■ Client Actions

□ Vendor Actions

M3 learning

Figure 26-2. ABC Company TripTik®.

Key Considerations

♦ A TripTik®is a mutual document. You will design it, but both parties are going on the trip, so both should participate in the development of the map. Leave blanks or sections for the prospect to fill out.

♦ A TripTik® ends at the prospect's Implementation Date (I-Date), not at the contract-signing date. Prospects care more about when they'll start using the product than when they agree to buy it. If possible, start with the I-Date and develop the map backward from there. That's how the prospect is thinking.

Some salespeople agree that the TripTik® sounds like a great tool and then fail to use it, since it requires some work to put one together. However, those who do use it report a 60 percent increase in sales.

It also gives you a competitive exclusive. Prospects are going to follow somebody's sales path. It may as well be yours. If you were in their shoes, wouldn't you rather take directions from somebody who shows you a map of the whole trip?

How to Prospect with It

The sooner you introduce the concept of the TripTik® the better. Here are some ideas to help you create the transfer of ownership:

♦ Introduce it when you end your first call:

"Mr. Rodriguez, this has been a very good meeting. If it would be okay with you, I'd like to lay out a few steps we can go through so you can figure out as quickly as possible if what we are talking about can really help you."

♦ Send a sample one:

"Mr. Rodriguez, this has been a good meeting. If it would be okay with you, I'd like to send you a map we have put together with some of our most loyal customers who were in a position similar to your position right now. We can go through it so you can figure out as quickly as possible if what we are talking about can really help you."

♦ Sell the next meeting:

"Mr. Rodriguez, this has been a good meeting. If it would be okay with you, at our next meeting we can discuss what you are trying to accomplish and map out the steps it will require for you to be able to make an informed decision. That way you can tell what the scope of this effort really will be."

The TripTik® is a great transfer-of-ownership tool. It gets prospects involved. It makes them think about the process they want to go through. And best of all, it makes them do that thinking with you, not with someone else.

Of all the tools in this book, the TripTik® is the one that can make the biggest difference in your prospecting/close ratio. Give it a try.

27

Two Paths:

Value vs. Solution

If you don't know where you're going, any road can take you there.

—Alice in Wonderland

At some point in the sales process you will come to a fork in the road. Two paths will diverge, and you'll have to choose one. Occasionally the choice will arise in an initial cold call, but more often it will come up during a second or subsequent call.

One fork is the solution path. The other is the value path.

The Solution Path

The solution path is all about what you can do for your prospects How will you help meet their needs? How will you help them solve a problem or seize an opportunity? How will you help them implement what you are selling so the result is happy customers?

You love the solution path. It's in your sweet spot. You get to have a features/benefits discussion—and that's what you've been trained to do. You're good at it.

You know you're on the solution path and progressing nicely when you hear the prospect say things like:

- This sounds great, tell me more.
- How can you do what you're describing?
- Can you do it this way?
- How would your solution fit into the "box" we've been defining?
- What does your new model do that this year's model can't?

There's nothing wrong with the solution path. But sometimes the sale needs to move in a different direction.

The Value Path

Most salespeople are far less comfortable with the value path. For them, it's an uncharted trail, outside their experience and training. So they tend to miss or ignore the signpost and continue trudging ahead on the solution path. But the value path is the one that vice presidents (Russians) and C-level executives (Greeks) want to go down. (See also Chapter 9.) If you miss the turn, you will leave them behind. Or rather, they'll leave you.

On the value path the focus is not so much on your product's specific features and benefits as on the business issues surrounding them: return on investment, time, risk, and brand. Comments you will hear from prospects who want to go down this path include:

- How will this save me/make me money?
- How much time will this service save me?
- What risks does this decision raise for the rest of my organization?
- How does this fit with our branding strategy?
- What makes you a vendor we'd want to partner with?

When to Use Which Path

Like salespeople, most prospects below the vice president level have been conditioned only to go down the solution path. And everyone, including executives, travels the solution path to some extent. It's a perfectly good path. You just need to know when to leave it behind—because both paths are often required to make a sale.

Use the solution path when:

♦ You are dealing with lower-level managers or product users.

♦ You are exploring something the prospect has never done before.

♦ You need to build rapport or excitement about the product before you can start down the value path (which is where you know you'll eventually have to go).

Use the value path when:

♦ You are dealing with vice presidents (Russians) or senior executives (Greeks).

♦ You want to gain access to senior executive (i.e., when you want lower-level prospects (Spaniards) to push you up the decision-maker ladder).

♦ You are getting interest on the solution path, but you need to establish another front.

♦ You know price is an objection.

♦ The prospect has a current process in place, and they're evaluating whether to change.

Ben was excited. After his initial thirty-second speech and some questions, the prospect had gotten seriously interested. She opened up and told him quite a bit about her plans. It sounded as if his products definitely could fit into her plans. Then the conversation hit a snag.

"It sounds quite interesting, Ben," the prospect said. "Why don't you send me some literature and we'll go from there?"

Fortunately, Ben recognized the classic "buyer takes control" line, and he was up to the challenge.

> Knowing that the prospect was a senior VP (Russian), he chose to turn the conversation onto the value path.
>
> "I'll be happy to do that," he said. "I have another quick question for you. What risks do you see in implementing a solution like this, and what might the return on an investment look like for your company?"
>
> "What do you mean?"
>
> "Well, most companies like yours look at what we offer from both the product-fit side, and the business-value side. I would also like to send you some information that will help in our next conversation. It shows the risks other companies have looked at when they implemented a solution like this and also some of the metrics they've used to measure ROI. If you look it over, then when we meet again you'll be in a better position to determine if this makes financial sense before we really dive deep into the functionality."

That's an example of a case where a salesperson chose to take a cold call down the value path in order to stay in control of the next step in the process. Ben will have plenty of time to travel the solution path with this vice president and with any specialists or submanagers (Spaniards) she may bring into the discussion.

Most often you'll hit the fork in the road during your second or third call on a prospect. But if you get an early opportunity to take the value path with a executive, be proactive and take it. It will shorten your sales cycle, keep you at the executive level, and let you sound like a potential business partner instead of just somebody peddling his wares. Willie Loman had no clue about the value path. But you do.

28

Putting the CART Before the Horse

It ain't over 'til it's over.

—Yogi Berra

Salesperson: *"This prospect never calls me back, and I don't want to keep bugging them. How many times should I call back—and how often?—before I just drop them?"*

Prospect: *"I have got to return that call I got the other day. It sounds interesting, but I just don't have time right now. Maybe I'll get back to them next week. Jeez, I really have to find more time for calls like these."*

What's peculiar about those thoughts is that salespeople all recognize the first one but don't really believe the second. Buyers can relate to the second, but don't believe that salespeople actually have qualms about bugging them.

We've said a lot about how to deal with prospects you *can* reach. What about the ones you have trouble reaching—the ones who don't return your calls?

Salespeople understand that they are crossing a line when they make a cold call. They worry about invading someone's space and want to be careful so they do not offend or get on the wrong side of the prospect. So let's talk about how to be aggressive but not pushy.

CART Rules of Cold Calling

When you are cold calling, the CART rules of sales and marketing apply:

1. Be **C**oncise.
2. Be **A**ctionable.
3. Be **R**epeatable.
4. Be **T**imely.

1. Be concise. Messages left or first interactions with the prospect should be short and sweet. That's why the thirty-second speech described in the "how-to's" section is so powerful. It's a great way for you to say what you need to say, and then listen and probe for opportunities.

2. Be actionable. Have in mind what you want the prospect to do. Cold calling works best when the salesperson is proactive and has an actionable next step to suggest. A little earlier we described a tool called the TripTik®. If you have one of those prepared and ready to send to prospects before you call, you'll never be at a loss for a next step.

Waiting for prospects to tell you what to do and where to go is tragic. Their suggestions in those areas aren't things your mom would want you to hear.

3. Be repeatable. If prospects hear the message again and again and again, three things happen.

- ♦ They believe it to be true.
- ♦ They start to build a rapport with the messenger.
- ♦ They want to be fair, so they believe they have a responsibility to do something.

If you are polite, informative, and sincere with your cold-calling efforts, your message will get through. Most of the time, salespeople blame themselves when prospects don't return their calls. "I must be doing it wrong." But the plain fact is that a lot of prospects are busy people and don't work on your time frame. Keep plugging.

4. Be timely. If you're just dialing random names from the phone book, the line between aggressive and pushy is razor thin. But if you've done your homework or otherwise have reason to believe that your target is a genuine prospect, follow the 1-3-5 Rule.

The 1-3-5 Rule

The 1-3-5 rule: For every one sales attempt, you should expect to leave at least three messages over a five-day time frame.

This accomplishes three goals. It will keep your message fresh in the prospect's mind. Your message will be consistent. And it will be delivered with due respect for the prospect's time.

If you finish the 1-3-5 cycle and don't get a response, you can drop the prospect for now. Or you can repeat the 1-3-5 cycle with a different message, which means six contacts over a ten-day window. Your message is getting through, and you are aggressively trying to reach the prospect without becoming a constant annoyance.

TIP: Mix up your 1-3-5 communications by leaving, say, one voice message, one e-mail, then another voice message. Choose fax, e-mail, phone, pager, letter, or personal visit—whatever mix of communication you feel will be most effective. It's that "sales as an art" thing again, right?

Remember CART. Be concise, actionable, repeatable, and timely, and your message will get through. The chances of a callback will improve tremendously, and you'll keep the sale alive.

29

It's All About You

The mind of man is capable of anything. Because everything is in it. All the past as well as all of the future.

—Joseph Conrad

Here we are at the end, and guess what: Prospecting is still not your favorite thing to do. On the other hand, we hope we have persuaded you that it's something you can have some fun with. It doesn't *have* to be as joyless as a trip to the dentist for a root canal.

If you follow the suggestions in this book, prospecting will be a lot more rewarding, too. You'll be successful far more often.

Here are a few final words of advice.

Make It Routine

Incorporate these tools and techniques into your everyday prospecting and cold-calling routine. The more you work at them, the better you will get. You will remember less than 15 percent of this book's lessons if you don't adopt them into your daily routine in the first twenty one days.

Set Goals

Write down some goals and post them where you have to see them daily. Yes, every self-help book tells you to do this—because it works.

From the tools and techniques we have offered, pick out the ones you like best and write them on Post-it® note—one technique per note. (Hey, you spent a few hours reading this book. Now make your time investment pay off.) Put the notes in your office where you'll see them. Scatter them on your bathroom mirror so you're reminded of them every morning. Make a bet with yourself that you'll incorporate X number of techniques into your routine each week until you're using all of your favorite ones. Maybe your goal is just one per week. The important thing is to get started and build some momentum.

Fight Change Resistance

Did we say that prospects hate change? Everybody hates change, and that includes you. If you want to get better at prospecting, your toughest opponent is inertia—the tendency to slip back into old habits. In the end, you will be the judge of whether you gave these tools a fair shake. Will you adopt them and adapt them to turn your prospecting efforts into art? Or will you read this book, say, "Yeah, I'll bet that would work for me," and then go right back to doing the things that made you hate prospecting in the first place?

Habits are hard to break. But don't give up the fight. The winner or the loser will be you. It's your choice and your effort that will determine what you take away from this book.

Really want to knock their socks off? Then go do it.

Index